effective
TEACHER ASSESSMENT

looking at children's learning in the primary classroom

Christine Mitchell and Valsa Koshy

Hodder & Stoughton
A MEMBER OF THE HODDER HEADLINE GROUP

The authors

Christine Mitchell is Lecturer in Education at the University of Exeter, and served as director of the joint ASE/ATM/MA/NATE working group *Primary Associations*. She has also had an active involvement in developing National Curriculum Key Stage 1 assessment and associated inset.

Valsa Koshy, formerly a primary maths consultant with ILEA, is Lecturer in Education at Brunel University, with a personal interest in working with gifted children.

Both authors have wide experience of primary teaching and education, and of delivering school-based inset.

British Library Cataloguing in Publication Data
Mitchell, Christine
   Effective Teacher Assessment: Looking at
   Children's Learning in the Primary
   Classroom
   I. Title II. Koshy, Valsa
   372.12

ISBN 0 340 65848 7

First published 1993
Second edition 1995
Impression number   10 9 8 7 6 5 4 3 2 1
Year   1999 1998 1997 1996 1995

Copyright © 1993, 1995 Christine Mitchell and Valsa Koshy

All rights reserved. No part of this publication may be reproduced in any form or by any means, electronic or mechanical, including photocopy, recording, or any information storage and retrieval system, without permission in writing from the publisher or under licence from the Copyright Licensing Agency Limited. Further details of such licences (for reprographic reproduction) may be obtained from the Copyright Licensing Agency Limited, of 90 Tottenham Court Road, London W1P 9HE.

Typeset by Wearset, Boldon, Tyne and Wear.
Printed in Great Britain for the educational publishing division of Hodder & Stoughton Ltd, 338 Euston Road, London NW1 3BH by Bath Press, Bath, Avon.

Contents

	Introduction	v
1	The National Curriculum Context	1
2	Gathering and Recording Assessment Information	10
3	Tuning into Formative Assessment: defining some working principles	22
4	The Planning–Learning–Assessing Cycle	33
5	Teacher Assessment in Action: looking at children's learning	47
6	Using the Formative Teacher Assessment Record	60
7	Organising for Effective Teacher Assessment	76
8	Sharing Assessment with Parents: recording and reporting	87
9	Developing a Whole-School Approach to Assessment	104
	Appendix	116
	Bibliography	121

Acknowledgements

We should like to thank the many teachers who worked with us in inservice courses on assessment; in particular, teachers and children from: Barnet, Devon, Ealing, Harrow, Hillingdon, Hounslow, Lambeth, Merton, Nottingham, Southwark, Surrey and Wandsworth.

We should also like to thank colleagues at the University of Exeter and the former West London Institute of Higher Education, particularly Richard Fox and Colin Mills, for their support.

We are very grateful for the technical and secretarial support given by Maggie Foster, Julie Hutchings, Margaret Rogers and Nigel Weaver in the production of this book.

We would like to thank the Open University for permission to draw on and develop material from Mitchell, C. (1991) 'Planning, Learning, Assessing: A Case Study' in *Mathematics in the Primary School* (Open University, E627).

We also thank the publishers for permission to reproduce copyright materials:

Figure 2.3, from *Checkpoints*, originally published by ILEA, now available from Harcourt Brace and Company Limited, copyright © Harcourt Brace and Company Limited.
Figure 6.1 ('The Fish Game') from *Nuffield Mathematics 2 Teachers' Handbook*, published by Heinemann Publishers (Oxford) Ltd.

Introduction

Effective Teacher Assessment offers a framework for looking closely at children's learning: we invite you to join with us in giving some serious attention to the question of what assessment has to offer to children's learning in the classroom and how it contributes to your own professional development.

We begin by outlining the assessment and reporting requirements of the 1988 Education Reform Act and the subsequent 1995 revisions which establish one particular backcloth and context for thinking about assessment. We are concerned not to be unduly or unnecessarily restricted by the statutory requirements, but aim to uncover and work through key ideas in assessment that will remain constant no matter how many changes in assessment legislation take place. In Chapter 2 we use case studies from practising teachers to illustrate alternative approaches to beginning assessment in the classroom; and in Chapter 3 go on to establish some working principles that are essential to healthy assessment practice.

The planning–learning–assessing cycle outlined in Chapter 4 highlights the central importance of formative assessment in supporting children's learning. This focus on formative assessment is developed further through the use of the Formative Teacher Assessment Record, which provides a structure for observing, analysing and making decisions about the way forward for children in their classroom learning. We spend some time in Chapters 5 and 6 defining the purposes and differences between each section of the Record, in the belief that observing and analysing children's learning are teacher skills that need to be nurtured and developed over a significant period of time.

Systematic use of the Formative Teacher Assessment Record (which may be freely copied for classroom and inset purposes) provides a way in to refining our understanding of individual children's learning needs, and at the same time helps us to identify professional strengths and limitations. We hope to provide you with enough guidance, support and encouragement to persevere with taking a closer look at both children's learning and your own classroom practices.

In Chapter 7 we consider aspects of classroom organisation that need to be confronted in order to ensure effective teacher assessment. Structuring daily/weekly routines and organising resources can be looked at and worked on fairly immediately. In the longer term, and at another level, making choices about organisation and management in the classroom can stimulate debate about the kinds of learning experiences on offer to children – the effectiveness of different kinds of teacher interventions, and how, and to what extent, children can be encouraged to take more responsibility for their learning.

Chapter 8 returns full circle to the statutory requirements for reporting outlined in Chapter 1. We suggest ways in which the Formative Teacher Assessment Record can be used as part of a record-keeping and reporting package. Finally, Chapter 9 offers some suggestions for developing a whole-school approach to assessment, and outlines six inservice sessions to complement and extend the ideas raised in previous chapters.

Effective Teacher Assessment is written as an interactive text and we hope you will pause in your reading to make a note of your own responses and, where possible, discuss and work through the points raised with colleagues in school. In this way, we hope you will feel empowered not only to complete the statutory requirements for assessment but, more importantly, to use observation and assessment to enhance and develop children's learning in the classroom.

1 The National Curriculum Context

The 1988 Education Reform Act delineated the content and assessment arrangements for a National Curriculum which covers nine subject areas for the primary age phase, in addition to Religious Education. Mathematics, English and Science are defined as **core subjects**, and Music, Physical Education, Art, History, Geography, and Design and Technology (plus Welsh, in Wales) as the other **foundation subjects**. Inevitably, the wider implications of implementing a National Curriculum emerged more fully as policies and practice developed from the legislation.

In 1993, Sir Ron Dearing was invited by the Secretary of State for Education to chair a review of the National Curriculum and its assessment procedures. Consequently, a revised, 'slimmer' version of each National Curriculum subject area was introduced into primary schools in August 1995.

As the National Curriculum continues to evolve and assessment procedures become more finely tuned, it is important to be clear as to the statutory requirements. Equally, it is important to keep the teaching–learning process central and ask: *'At the end of the day, what's important in this for me as the teacher, and for the children as learners in my care?'*

In this chapter we identify the essential and most constant features of the assessment legislation, leaving to one side details of administrative routines that are likely to vary from year to year. We take a look at the influence of the Task Group on Assessment and Testing (1988) and the Dearing Review (1993) on the assessment of National Curriculum mathematics, science and English in primary schools, and focus on the different kinds and purposes of assessment to provide a framework for subsequent chapters.

National Curriculum assessment

National Curriculum assessment for mathematics, science and English requires teachers to take responsibility for two kinds of assessment:

- **teacher assessment** (TA) of every attainment target, based on the children's everyday learning experiences, taken over a period of time and summarised by level at the end of each Key Stage;
- **standard assessment**, which is teacher assessment taking place within a specified period of time (Years 2 and 6), using standard assessment tests and tasks (SATs). Key Stage 1 SATs test aspects of English and mathematics. Key Stage 2 SATs test aspects of English, mathematics and science.

The task for teachers of pupils in their final year of Key Stage 1 (Year 2) and Key Stage 2 (Year 6) involves:

- providing a summary of teacher assessment in the three core subjects by a specified time;
- administering and recording the results of SATs in the appropriate core subjects by a specified time.

Although, in practice, Y2 and Y6 teachers have responsibility for major elements of the national assessment process, the requirements for teacher assessment allow for assessments that have been made *throughout* the Key Stage to be taken into account at the end of the Key Stage. In this way, teacher assessments made in years R, Y1, Y3, Y4 and Y5 can make a significant contribution to any summaries prepared by the Y2 and Y6 teachers.

One of the themes addressed in subsequent chapters is *how* you and your colleagues can develop a systematic, whole-school approach to teacher assessment which both enhances teaching and learning and provides appropriate information for Y2 and Y6 teachers to feel confident enough to complete the statutory requirements at the end of the Key Stage. We suggest that the approach we take to formative teacher assessment for mathematics, science and English can equally well be applied to the assessment of the foundation subjects. Developing skills and confidence in everyday teacher assessment will also enhance the administration of standard assessment tasks or tests, whatever form these take in succeeding years.

The influence of the Task Group on Assessment and Testing

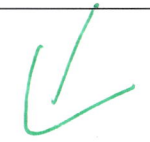

The two elements of teacher assessment and standard assessment had their origins in one of the recommendations made in the *National Curriculum: Task Group on Assessment and Testing (TGAT) Report* (1988):

> *The national assessment system should be based on consideration of teachers' ratings and standardised tasks.*

(para. 63)

TGAT had been asked by the Secretary of State to consider how to assess and report on children's progress across the National Curriculum subjects. The TGAT model for assessment and reporting also recommended that:

- the ages for national assessment and reporting should be 7, 11, 14, and 16 (para. 92);
- ten levels of achievement for each subject should be defined (para. 101);
- a wide range of testing approaches should be used and these should be called 'standard assessment tasks' (para. 50).

Each of the recommendations has established a niche in the discourse about the national assessment system. Consider for a moment how the recommendations have influenced your own thinking and the story you have to tell about assessment and learning. On a scale of 0–10 (with 0 = not at all and 10 = a lot!), how much does the 'standard' aspect of national assessment (SATs) feature in any discussion you have with colleagues? And what about the 'levels'? TGAT identified that the levels of attainment for most seven-year-olds would be 1 to 3, with the majority of pupils at level 2. For nearly all eleven-year-olds, TGAT suggested the range would be amongst levels 3, 4 and 5, with level 4 occurring most frequently.

The TGAT rationale for assigning numbers to different levels of achievement was to make the whole area of *reporting* achievement more manageable. Following this model through, it would seem that 'levels' need only take on a high profile at times when reporting to parents and others is required.

More TGAT influences

The Task Group took special care to highlight how their recommendations for a national assessment system differ from many previous and standardised tests. Two (out of four) general criteria listed by TGAT are particularly helpful in this context:

+ the assessment results should give direct information about pupils' achievement in relation to objectives: they should be criterion-referenced;
+ the results should provide a basis for decisions about pupils' further learning needs: they should be formative.

(para. 5)

The Task Group recommended that the assessment system should be **criterion-referenced** and focus on what children *can do* in direct relation to what they are being taught. In this way, the assessment is directly linked with the National Curriculum, which provides the *content* focus for learning and teaching. For both TA and SATs, the *level descriptions* in each subject area now provide the criteria for assessing each child's level of attainment. This provides a strong contrast to the norm-referenced testing previously used for assessment in many primary schools. **Norm-referenced** assessment involves assessing children on a scale that has been specially devised by using the performance of a sample group of children to provide the range of standard performance: the 'norm'. Using norm-referenced tests is a way of comparing children with one another. TGAT stated quite clearly that '. . . *in the system proposed, norm-referenced tests do not have a role'*. Nevertheless, it's hard to escape completely from norm-referencing, as the setting up of a criterion-referenced system involves the establishment of criteria for assessing children's learning which incidentally involves 'norms' and values of one kind or another.

The second of the TGAT general criteria highlights the link between assessing children and planning their future learning. This **formative** aspect of assessment is the central theme developed throughout this book, and has been strongly endorsed in the advice offered by the DFE and the School Curriculum and Assessment Authority (SCAA) in various publications.

TGAT identified the **summative** aspect of assessment as mainly taking place for sixteen-year-olds as they complete their statutory schooling. Certainly, for seven- and eleven-year-olds the summative function of the assessment procedure necessarily has a very short shelf-life, as any summary of achievement made at these ages is completed in the midst of ongoing learning and schooling. Throughout the primary and secondary phases children will learn in all kinds of leaps, bounds and untidy ways that cannot be conveyed in a neat system of numbered levels. The summative element of the assessment procedure at 7, 11, 14 (and to some extent 16) therefore needs to be seen as a snapshot at a particular moment, and like all good holiday snapshots has a particular story to tell. Of course, the story has moved on even before the prints are developed.

The different purposes of assessment

Assessing children's learning can take place in a variety of ways across a continuum from very informal, spontaneous, almost 'chance' classroom observations, through to formal, highly structured, standardised testing. Whichever approach to assessment is used, the information gathered can be used in a number of ways which are different yet centrally linked to a basic assumption that *'Assessment is at the heart of the process of promoting children's learning'* (TGAT, para. 3).

TGAT identified the importance of both the formative and summative *purposes* of assessment. **Formative** assessment involves using assessment to inform the choices and plans you make concerning the way forward for individual children or a group of children: sharing the assessment information with the children may enable you to work together to identify and make explicit the next learning goals. On some occasions, and for some children, further **diagnostic** assessments may be necessary in order to pinpoint the most helpful learning pathway.

Summative assessment, as we have already noted, provides a summary of achievement up to a particular moment in time. Sometimes the same assessment information is used for both formative and summative purposes, whereas in examinations such as GCSE at 16+, the assessments are designed solely for summative purposes.

Assessments can also be used to **evaluate** the effectiveness of classroom activities and the curriculum as a whole. Assessment data across a class or school or LEA can be aggregated and any significant trends monitored. The logical next stage would be to consider the implications for future resourcing and in-service education. Sharing the information available from assessments and evaluations can help to develop meaningful channels of communication between children, parents and teachers. There are minimal legal requirements for reporting to parents that can establish a baseline. In outline, the Regulations require:

♦ at least one written report every school year for each pupil to be sent to parents at a time of the school's choosing;

- at some point during the year parents must be sent information about their child's progress in the following areas:
  - all National Curriculum subjects studied,
  - all other subjects and activities,

  The report should also include:
  - an attendance and general progress comment,
  - the arrangements to discuss the report with the school.

At the end of a Key Stage parents have a legal right to be given written information on the National Curriculum levels achieved by their child. And so, parents with children in either Y2 or Y6 will receive information on the levels achieved during the SATs alongside the levels awarded as a result of TA gathered during preceding years. In addition, at the end of Key Stage 1 parents are entitled to two different kinds of comparative information:

- how their child's National Curriculum achievements compares to the achievements of other children in the same school; and
- national comparisons of National Curriculum achievements.

The idea of recording and reporting progress by means of a Record of Achievement for individual pupils is noted in the TGAT recommendations (para. 162) and in subsequent guidance provided by the School Examinations and Assessment Council (SEAC): *Records of Achievement in Primary Schools* (1990). We take a look at the potential of Records of Achievement in Chapter 9.

Finally, assessment procedures and processes can be used as a focus for **professional development** and growth (DES 1988). This particular purpose underpins the approach we have taken throughout the book, which is to invite you to reflect and engage with the material in each chapter, in the light of your own professional experience and particular school context. We focus attention on the *formative* aspects of assessment, in the belief that formative assessment is fundamental to effective teacher assessment. We then follow through detailed examples from one system of formative teacher assessment which has proved effective, and highlight aspects of classroom practice that can usefully be reviewed throughout the process of developing a systematic approach to teacher assessment.

The influence of the Dearing Review

Support for the enhancement of teacher assessment was a central theme of both reports by Sir Ron Dearing (*The National*

English NC (1991) Speaking and Listening, Level 4 (*statements of attainment*) Pupils should be able to:	English NC (1995) Speaking and Listening, Level 4 (*level description*)
(a) give a detailed oral account of an event, or something that has been learned in the classroom, or explain with reasons why a particular course of action was taken. (b) ask and respond to questions in a range of situations with increased confidence. (c) take part as speakers and listeners in a group discussion or activity, expressing a personal view and commenting constructively on what is being discussed or experienced. (d) participate in a presentation.	Pupils talk and listen with confidence in an increasing range of contexts. Their talk is adapted to the purpose: developing ideas thoughtfully, describing events and conveying their opinions clearly. In discussion, they listen carefully making contributions and asking questions that are responsive to others' ideas and views. They use appropriately some of the core features of standard English vocabulary and grammar.

Figure 1.1 *The 1991 and 1995 National Curriculum assessment criteria for English, Speaking and Listening, Level 4*

Curriculum and its Assessment, July and December 1993) resulting from his review of the National Curriculum. He was concerned to give equal standing to teacher assessment and the results of national tests, and highlighted the need for *'soundly based'* teacher assessment. At the same time, Dearing recognised the need to make the whole National Curriculum assessment process more manageable by reducing the amount of material teachers needed to make assessment judgements on.

As a consequence of the Dearing Review (1993) the revised National Curriculum presents **level descriptions** of the kinds of performances expected of children at particular levels of the National Curriculum. Teachers are required to look for the level description which *'best fits'* the individual child's performance. The level descriptions compare favourably with the previous National Curriculum assessment procedure whereby teachers were matching children's performance against a large number of individual *statements of attainment*.

Fig 1.1 illustrates the change by reference to both the 1991 and the revised 1995 English National Curriculum at Level 4 of the Speaking and Listening Attainment Target. Looking for and judging which description best fits a child's performance allows teachers to use their *professional judgement* and to develop a different kind of rigour within the assessment system. Level descriptions also acknowledge implicitly that children's learning and attainment are not always clear-cut, hard-and-fast commodities that can be checked off against a ticklist in a straightforward fashion – there are some fuzzy, uncertain edges which can be accommodated within the broader boundaries of the level descriptions.

The following chapters aim to help you to develop soundly based professional judgements and to give you confidence in the assessments you make concerning children's learning, including any decisions you may need to make at the end of Key Stages in relation to 'best fit' level descriptions.

In summary:

- assessment is an integral part of the National Curriculum and involves teacher assessment and standard assessment;
- at the end of the Key Stage, teachers are responsible for providing a report of the teacher assessment (TA) that has taken place throughout the Key Stage as part of ongoing classroom practice, as well as
- administering Standard Assessment Tests (SATs) in Y2 and Y6 and reporting the SAT results;
- an annual written report of children's achievement in all National Curriculum subjects should be provided for parents. At the end of Key Stages 1 and 2, the reports should identify levels of attainment in each subject;
- LEAs are responsible for the local administration of the national assessment system;
- SCAA is responsible for monitoring and evaluating the national assessment procedures, approving SATs and offering guidance on all aspects of the curriculum, assessment and reporting.

Year Group	Age	Assessment	Reporting
Y1		ongoing TA	all NC subjects other activites
Y2	7	ongoing TA summary of TA SATs	all NC subjects other activities results of TA/SATs
Y3		ongoing TA	all NC subjects other activities
Y4		ongoing TA	all NC subjects other activities
Y5		ongoing TA	all NC subjects other activities
Y6	11	ongoing TA summary of TA SATs	all NC subjects other activities results of TA/SATs

Figure 1.2 *Summary of national assessment requirements*

2 Gathering and Recording Assessment Information

In this chapter we look at some of the different ways teachers collect and record information about children's learning, and consider some of the advantages and disadvantages of particular approaches. Five case studies represent a range of possibilities for assessing the three core subjects of mathematics, science and English. The case studies were gathered in the course of inset work in a variety of Key Stage 1 and Key Stage 2 classrooms.

A number of techniques were used by the teachers to collect information about the children, and the records they kept ranged from *'it is all up here in my head, I don't write anything down'* to keeping copious notes and finding the whole process cumbersome. Some of the approaches may be familiar to you, so take some time to revisit each method in terms of the different *purposes of* assessment – formative, summative, evaluative and for professional development – outlined in Chapter 1.

School A

Using a markbook

This school has no specific whole-school assessment policy at present. Each teacher uses a personal record-keeping system. Penny, a Y4 class teacher, describes her assessment system as based on her entries in her markbook. She does not *'consciously gather information about the children'*, but completes her markbook *'when there is anything to record'*. Penny's markbook entries consist of a record of the books which children read, page numbers completed from the published maths scheme she uses, and a list of other activities, such as art work, computers and making music. Penny explains her ticks as:

❛ *useful, because I can monitor how the children are doing. A tick means they have completed the task given. As their teacher I need to do that. Notes about the reading books and completed maths pages are passed on to their new teacher. I write some comments about their work and attitudes for the parents' records at the end of the year.* ❜

When asked if she was happy about her assessment system, Penny expressed some uneasiness:

❛ *Not all of it. For a start I need to have a ticklist for the science work we do. No. I am not happy, but I will have to stick to it until someone comes up with something better and convinces me that it is better.* ❜

There seems to be some confusion in Penny's mind between assessment and record-keeping. There is no conscious gathering of evidence to demonstrate what children know or understand, neither are specific learning difficulties recorded. Penny certainly makes sure that children work hard and everybody gets a chance to do all of the activities, but the records do not inform anyone about how the children approach their work. Compiling a list of books read by the child does not indicate anything about the child's attitude to reading, whether she enjoys reading or whether she understands what she reads, neither are the strategies she uses during reading identified.

In this model, the only evidence of *sharing* the teacher's assessment of the child's attainment with the individual concerned is found in the form of ticks or an occasional comment in the maths or writing book about the work:

Well done, but I am not sure this is your best.

This is good stuff.

Neat, tidy work.

Could do more if you tried.

Hard work – 10 team points.

School B

Observing children

Close observation of children is the way that School B recommends that teachers should collect information about the children.

Fiona, who teaches a Y5 class, shared one of her observation sheets. Children are observed when they are engaged in different activities. Each day children are given an assignment sheet:

GROUP	DATE ....
MATHS	Handshakes problem with your red group
READING	Continue with the book Find time to read to me today
WRITING	Answer 'Flight' questions

Fiona observes the children and listens to them while they are engaged in solving the 'handshake problem':

> If every child in this class shook hands with everyone else, just once, how many handshakes will take place?

The notes she made are shown in Figure 2.1.

Fiona explains that these observations are carried out and recorded whenever she can manage it. These sheets are filed away with any recording the child has done attached to it. Also attached to the observation sheets is Fiona's own evaluation of the task:

> *I think children found the problem-solving task confusing. Maybe I expected too much. Maybe I should have asked: 'how many handshakes would take place at your table' first, then extended it if they succeeded.*

Observation sheets are done for both science and maths. Writing tasks are marked and filed away with some comments written on them.

The observation notes are studied and taken into account in planning the next lesson, which helps Fiona to improve her

> Darren: Works fast, enjoys the work but not happy to work with any one else. Worked out that it would be 15 handshakes for 5 people and started day-dreaming.
>
> Natasha: Changed attitude!! Actually smiled at me today (!), as she was walking to the sink. But work was slow. Chatted to Adrian most of the time.
>
> Adrian: As usual no work — Chat, Chat...
>
> Abu: Shouted out 400 handshakes then started scribbling, scribbled for a long time. — no system!
>
> Mandip: Estimated 400 at first. I can see why he thought that. Very pleasing to see him working hard....

Figure 2.1 *Fiona's observation notes*

own teaching strategies. Fiona admits that it is very difficult to sift through all that paper and gather relevant information. Reflecting on her assessment and recording system, Fiona expressed some concerns. Although she abandoned writing at least a page of A4 about each child using her observations, she still finds it difficult to write notes every single day. Fiona observed:

❛ *We only have a certain amount of energy. If so much of it is given to writing down comments, I feel that something else will suffer. If the quality of the teaching is what goes, then it is a great shame.* ❜

Fiona was critical about her notes too. She felt that her comments were more about the children's attitudes and some process skills: *'I need to think about some way of assessing and recording the skills and concepts such as adding and taking away and multiplication.'* When asked if she ever told the children what she wrote about them, she explained that initially she had not, but now she does tell them occasionally:

> *It really is the decent thing to do, children were very pleased that I was writing about them. It makes them feel important.*

Fiona's assessment system seems to have several positive features that are worth reflecting upon. It is based on close observation of what the children do, and helps Fiona to evaluate her own teaching. Changes in her teaching methods are the result of her own power of critical analysis and reflection. Perhaps Fiona needs to think about structuring her observations more efficiently and completing the observation sheets less frequently but more thoroughly. She will need to reflect on how she can be more precise in what she writes by focusing on specific outcomes. What is important is the *quality* of her assessment notes, not the quantity. She could still collect children's recorded work (see Mandip's work in Figure 2.2) and analyse it in a more structured way using the Formative Teacher Assessment Record approach suggested in Chapters 5 and 6.

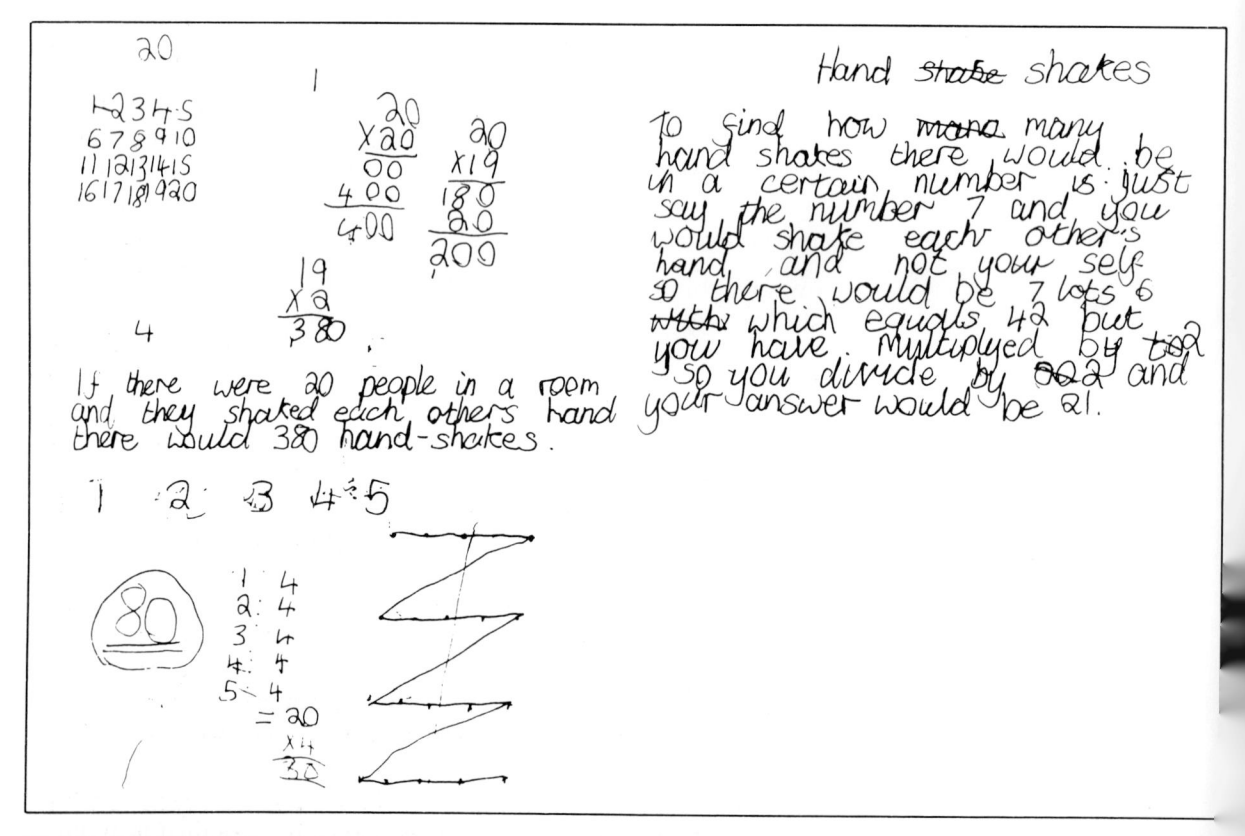

Figure 2.2 *Mandip's work*

School C

Administering tests

David teaches a Y3 class in a school where the assessment system currently in operation consists of the use of commercially produced tests. The tests are provided by the Local Education Authority and administered annually by the class teachers in May. Reading is tested using a standardised test which gives a raw score and a reading age which is used to monitor progress and to make comparisons between pupils. The mathematics test consists of sums and word problems. These tests are sometimes administered orally to avoid putting children with reading difficulties at a disadvantage. Tests are marked and a score is given to each child. The results are shared with the parents. The test paper is passed on to the new teacher, then filed away.

When asked if these tests were the *only* means of collecting information about the children's learning. David's reply was:

> *Formally, yes, that is the only form of assessment. But we mark the children's work in their books. We have a syllabus and the children are taught all the topics before they are tested. They are also encouraged to read and talk to adults.*

David defends the use of tests in terms of their being simple to administer and providing a summative record. He feels these tests at the end of each year are important because SATs are only administered at the *end* of Key Stages. He insists that informal assessment is going on all the time. He admits, however, to feeling somewhat uneasy about the nature of the standard assessment tasks.

A system based on assigning a score for reading encounters similar difficulties to Penny's example in School A. Although a reading score may be helpful in certain contexts, the amount of meaningful information it is possible to convey to parents and children via a score – or, indeed, an attainment target or subject 'level' – is limited. Numbers neither provide immediate access to the child's interest in reading nor highlight the strategies used by individual readers.

In the case of mathematics, tests can assess, to some extent, understanding of concepts and skills in mathematical topics and identify difficulties experienced by children. But the teacher will need to supplement this information with individual interviews and observations to find out the causes and nature of the difficulties experienced by children, and probe into any misconceptions held by them. The type of tests used by David's school, which only gave evidence of learning basic skills, does not give the teacher any insight into the child's development of mathematical processes, or say anything about his or her ability to work in groups or communicate mathematical ideas.

A written test cannot provide a teacher with an ongoing profile of the child's development. Only by making a conscious effort to gather evidence of the child's learning and performance at different times in the year would David be able to build a coherent profile of his children's progress. Evidence collected throughout the year would help David to plan the next stage in the child's learning. The end-of-year test results come too late for him to make use of them in his daily planning.

School D

The Primary Language Record and Checkpoints

In this school a commercially produced assessment format, the *Primary Language Record* (Barrs *et al.* 1988), is used to assess children's language work. Assessment is continuous, and recording is done at different stages during the year. The record encourages the teacher to discuss with parents the children's interests and achievements in reading, speaking and writing. Equal opportunities play an important part in the assessment system and advice is given on how to assess children who are bilingual. The children are actively involved in the assessment process by commenting on their work and in selecting the samples of work to be kept. These pieces of work are used as evidence of children's development as writers.

Claire, who teaches a Y5 class, is full of praise for the *Primary Language Record*. She admits to having difficulties initially in organising her time to complete the record, but now that she is accustomed to it, she finds it very useful. Reflecting on why she likes the *Primary Language Record*, Claire comments:

> *I suppose I like it because it is thorough and very structured. It also involves the parents in record-keeping. It would be nice to have a structured system which could be used for all subjects.*

For assessing mathematics, Claire uses *Checkpoints* (ILEA). When the Checkpoints were bought by the school, about ten years ago, they were only used as reference material. In the wake of the Education Reform Act, the need to use some structured material for assessment made the school go back to the 'box of cards'.

The cards provide tasks to be used to assess children either individually or in groups. By observing and listening to the children, the teacher makes a judgement about their knowledge and understanding of mathematical concepts and skills. The

'What may happen' section gives guidance on the assessment and 'Suggestions for children who need more help' (on the reverse) point you in the right direction for future action.

❛ *It helps me a great deal to use these cards. I always found maths teaching difficult and am afraid of passing this on. The Checkpoints card gives me some background information about the mathematical concepts I have to teach.* ❜

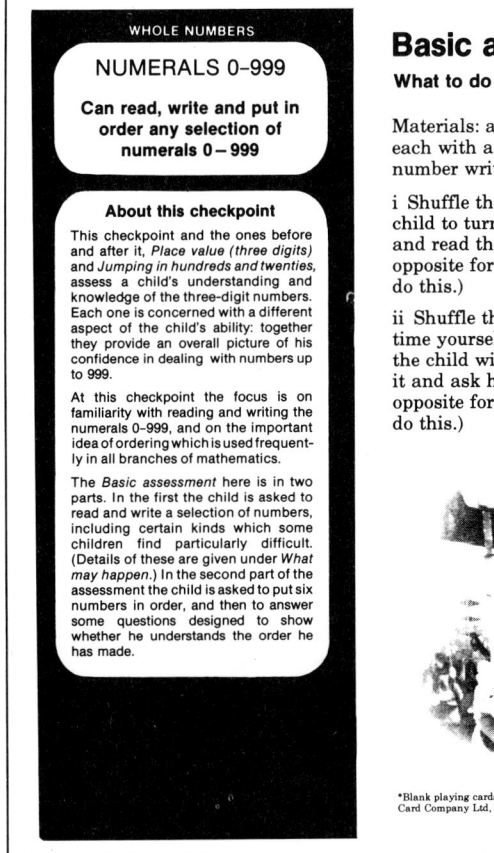

WHOLE NUMBERS
NUMERALS 0–999
Can read, write and put in order any selection of numerals 0–999

About this checkpoint

This checkpoint and the ones before and after it, *Place value (three digits)* and *Jumping in hundreds and twenties*, assess a child's understanding and knowledge of the three-digit numbers. Each one is concerned with a different aspect of the child's ability: together they provide an overall picture of his confidence in dealing with numbers up to 999.

At this checkpoint the focus is on familiarity with reading and writing the numerals 0–999, and on the important idea of ordering which is used frequently in all branches of mathematics.

The *Basic assessment* here is in two parts. In the first part the child is asked to read and write a selection of numbers, including certain kinds which some children find particularly difficult. (Details of these are given under *What may happen*.) In the second part of the assessment the child is asked to put six numbers in order, and then to answer some questions designed to show whether he understands the order he has made.

Basic assessment

Whole numbers CARD 9

What to do

Materials: a pack of about 50 cards, each with a different three-digit number written on it*

i Shuffle the cards and ask the child to turn over one at a time and read the number on it. (See opposite for how many times to do this.)

ii Shuffle the cards, take one at a time yourself, read the number to the child without letting him see it and ask him to write it. (See opposite for how many times to do this.)

What may happen

In both these activities enough cards should be used for you to assess the child on each of the following:
- a number with zero in the tens place (like 608)
- a number with zero in the ones place (like 870)
- a 'teen' number (like 911)
- about four other numbers

A child who is ready for this part of the assessment should be able to read and write correctly all the numbers that you give him. He may make, say, just one error but he should be able to correct it when asked.

A child who is not ready for this part of the assessment will make several errors. If any of these involve confusing one digit with another then he should be assessed at *Place value (three digits)* to make sure that he understands the basic principles of place value (see *Background mathematical information*).

continued overleaf

*Blank playing cards are available from Waddingtons Playing Card Company Ltd, Wakefield Road, Leeds

Figure 2.3 *A Checkpoints card*

Copyright © Harcourt Brace and Company Ltd

Claire only uses some cards, like the one in Figure 2.3 which assesses children's understanding of number. The assessment is recorded on a sheet which is based on the National Curriculum. The concepts specifically assessed by *Checkpoints* are very close to the statements of attainment in the National Curriculum. The school's objective is to develop a bank of maths assessment activities to be used for unaided work by the children to provide a focus for close observation. The teachers told us that they are aware that *Checkpoints* do not give much opportunity for assessing *process* skills and problem-solving. The teachers also find the activities in the *Graded Assessment of Mathematics* (GAIM) scheme useful, as they give pointers as to what to look for during the assessment.

School D is attempting to provide an assessment system which strives for a balance between assessing processes, skills and concepts, using good tasks and involving parents and children in the assessment process. Time and energy is expended towards finding tasks for assessment purposes. An alternative approach would be to look for activities which are rich in their potential to promote learning, and to allow the assessment to follow from the learning focus.

School E

Using a checklist

Jamal teaches seven-year-olds. His school's assessment policy is based on the principle that the collection of evidence about children's learning is a continuous process. Jamal explained that an example of an assessment opportunity could be a class discussion. Jamal discusses a topic with the children before he teaches it. He believes that this initial discussion helps him to 'gauge' where the children are in their understanding of concepts, to help him to plan more efficiently:

Science Record

Name:
Year:

Programmes of study ⟶

	1 a b c d e	2 a b c d e f g h	3 a b c d e f g
Experimental and Investigative Science	✓ ✓ ✓ ✓ ✓	✓	
Life Processes and Living Things	✓ ✓		
Materials and their Properties	✓ ✓ ✓	✓ ✓ ✓	
Physical Processes	✓ ✓ ✓ ✓ ✓	✓ ✓	

Figure 2.4 *Checklist for science*

Children learn outside school, they read about things in books, see television programmes and listen to adults. It is important that this is taken into account. A discussion at the start helps me to do that; it also activates children's existing framework of knowledge before new experiences are given.

Jamal believes that plenary sessions with groups of children, or with the whole class after a topic is dealt with, also provide him with assessment opportunities. The following is an extract from a discussion he conducted with the children after learning about electricity, in response to his question: *'So what have we found out?'*

Children's responses:

- 'It gives us light'
- 'A battery has two terminals.'
- 'You need a wire, batteries and a bulb to make light.'
- 'The bulb will only light when you complete a circuit.'
- 'If you cut the wire in the middle you don't get a light.'
- 'Only a wire will pass electricity through, cotton won't.'

Jamal claims that these statements made by the children help him to assess the children's knowledge. However, he admits that he only makes a mental note of who said what and quite often forgets who said what before he writes anything down.

How does Jamal record the information he collects from children? The school has checklists for mathematics and science like the ones shown in Figures 2.4 and 2.5. The statements of attainment are listed, and once a week Jamal ticks the list from his memory of what children said and did.

	Mathematics Record			
Name: Year	Programmes of study →			
	1 a b c d	2 a b c d	3 a b c d e f g h	4 a b c
Using and Applying Mathematics	✓ ✓	✓ ✓ ✓		
Number	✓ ✓ ✓ ✓	✓ ✓ ✓		
Shape, Space and Measures	✓ ✓	✓ ✓		
Handling Data	✓ ✓ ✓			

Figure 2.5 *Checklist for mathematics*

There is no checklist for English, except a reading record of books chosen by the children.

Checklists like the ones illustrated here seem to be the most common form of recording children's learning outcomes in schools. Teachers who used them justified their use because they were 'simple', 'less time-consuming' and 'because they relate easily to the programmes of study'. Nevertheless, teachers we interviewed did show concern that checklists were inadequate to assess process skills, attitudes to work and communication skills. Concern was also expressed that checklists did not offer any opportunities to show children's increase in confidence or competence in doing work. Additionally, many feel that checklists do not support the teacher at parents' evenings or in any way help communication with parents. Children's *self*-assessment was not given a high profile unless teachers had begun to focus on developing portfolios of children's work.

Developing portfolios

A number of schools we visited were developing the idea of children having a portfolio of their own work. A portfolio is a folder or file where samples of children's work are kept. All the teachers who had portfolios in their classrooms acknowledged the positive influence these had on children's learning. Different types of work samples were kept by children – writing, drawings, self-made games, certificates and poems. Pieces of work were dated, and some children wrote down their own assessment of their work; teachers added their comments. Some examples of children's work kept in personal portfolios can be found in Chapter 8.

Each of the different approaches to gathering and recording information about children's learning and achievement outlined in this chapter has its own story to tell about assessment in the classroom. The following chapters of this book are designed to help you to develop and shape your own skills and story about teacher assessment.

3 Tuning into Formative Assessment: defining some working principles

❛ *The word 'assessment' has the effect of making my hair stand on end now, simply because there seem to be no answers forthcoming to questions which I and many colleagues are asking.* ❜

(Liz, primary teacher)

Assessment is a complex business guaranteed to evoke some pretty strong emotions and responses. It is certainly frustrating, if not infuriating, when questions are left unanswered and when responses are far from clear-cut. However, one of the prevalent myths associated with the assessment debate is that there are people 'out there somewhere' with a sure-fire formula for success – not so! Nevertheless, there *are* productive ways forward. An essential first step is to let go of the idea that 'they' know or that there is only one definitive approach to assessment. This releases some energy for working through a range of possibilities, identifying the key considerations for you and your classroom, and responding to the 'global' questions by starting with yourself and developing your own understanding of assessment practices.

A reminder

It is important not to confuse procedures which are designed to satisfy the *administrative* requirements of National Curriculum assessment with procedures and processes that endeavour to make sense of the idea that assessment promotes children's learning. In theory, it's possible that the two are not mutually exclusive, but often, in practice, more time is given to secretarial record-keeping tasks, leaving relatively little time for exploring the more vital question of how assessment can enhance learning in the classroom. We want to redress the balance and bring the formative and professional development aspects of assessment sharply into focus.

Starting with yourself:
What do I bring to the assessment situation?

We all bring our own preconceptions, emotions and experiences to the assessment situation. One way of identifying and exploring these is to begin by completing the following statements:

'One thing I'm looking forward to about assessment is . . .'
'One thing I'm worried about assessment is . . '

If you can, ask a colleague to complete the exercise as well. Take some time to discuss your individual responses together. Don't look for solutions yet: stay with exploring what's behind each sentence for *you*. Compare your responses to the following examples from primary teachers:

One thing I'm looking forward to about assessment is . .

developing a fair system that is user friendly and can be shared by others.

that every child will have a fair chance of getting my attention.

it may help me to evaluate myself more clearly and enable me to adapt my teaching techniques.

finding out new ways of exploring the development of an individual child.

it will help to focus my attention more closely on the particular-both child and task.

One thing I'm worried about assessment is . . .

having the time to give to all 33 children
and to carry out a fair system.

that it might take the 'fun' out of teaching and learning.

just getting it underway.

that having a large number of children I will not have the time or opportunity to evaluate the progress of each individual child.

have I done justice to the children in question?

how will my assessment be received by others?

As teachers, we have all been on the receiving end of both positive and negative experiences of assessment, and this in turn will influence how we feel and respond to the current requirements. It's worth spending a few minutes reviewing your own personal assessment 'history' from five years old onwards! Try this listening exercise with a friend:

Listening exercise

Take it in turns to be A and B. First of all, A spends five minutes listening to B, who recounts her memories of being assessed. It is important for A only to listen (supportive nods, smiles and grunts are okay) and to try to spot the various emotions that are around in B's history. Moments of silence will encourage memories to surface. After five minutes, A recaps on the significant points of what B has said and tries to identify the various emotions around. The roles are then reversed and the exercise repeated, with B listening to A.

Both this and the previous exercise should help to reveal some of what you personally bring to any debate on assessment. You may then like to explore one stage further and consider how your past experiences influence you as an assessor. Alternatively, you may like to consider the implications of the following examples:

MEMORY 1

A lesson in home economics wherein each shepherd's pie was assessed against all the other shepherd's pies produced during that day. All the pies were displayed on the front table and the teacher began her inspection. It was the usual practice of this particular teacher to comment on individual items or groups of items that displayed similar qualities and to systematically remove all items of inferior quality. In this way, only the 'best' items were assigned a B+ and remained on display for the rest of the day. On this particular occasion, my shepherd's pie was there amongst the final four but the teacher, after further public debate, declared that although it was "almost there" the decorative piping of the potato was not quite perfect. The pie was duly removed.

MEMORY 2

End of year primary school tests. Mark obtained for writing an imaginative story: 25 out of 25, maximum. Teacher's verbal response: "That's the best story I've ever read".

Starting with children: where to begin?

Close your eyes for a moment and let your thoughts drift around the children in your class. Focus in on one child. What thoughts immediately come to mind? Jot them down on a piece of paper. Try a couple of examples for yourself before you read on. The responses in Figure 3.1 are from teachers who have tried this exercise.

Typically, most 'first thoughts' descriptions of individual children tend to highlight aspects of personality or behaviour patterns. This is bound to be the case when part of the daily life of the teacher involves managing 30+ personalities in order to maintain relative harmony and to encourage a productive learning environment! Nevertheless, if we are concerned to develop formative procedures, it is necessary to move beyond personality and associated behaviours to identify intellectual development and learning behaviours. By this, we do not mean to suggest that the two domains are mutually exclusive. On the contrary, the inter-relationship between affect and intellect is

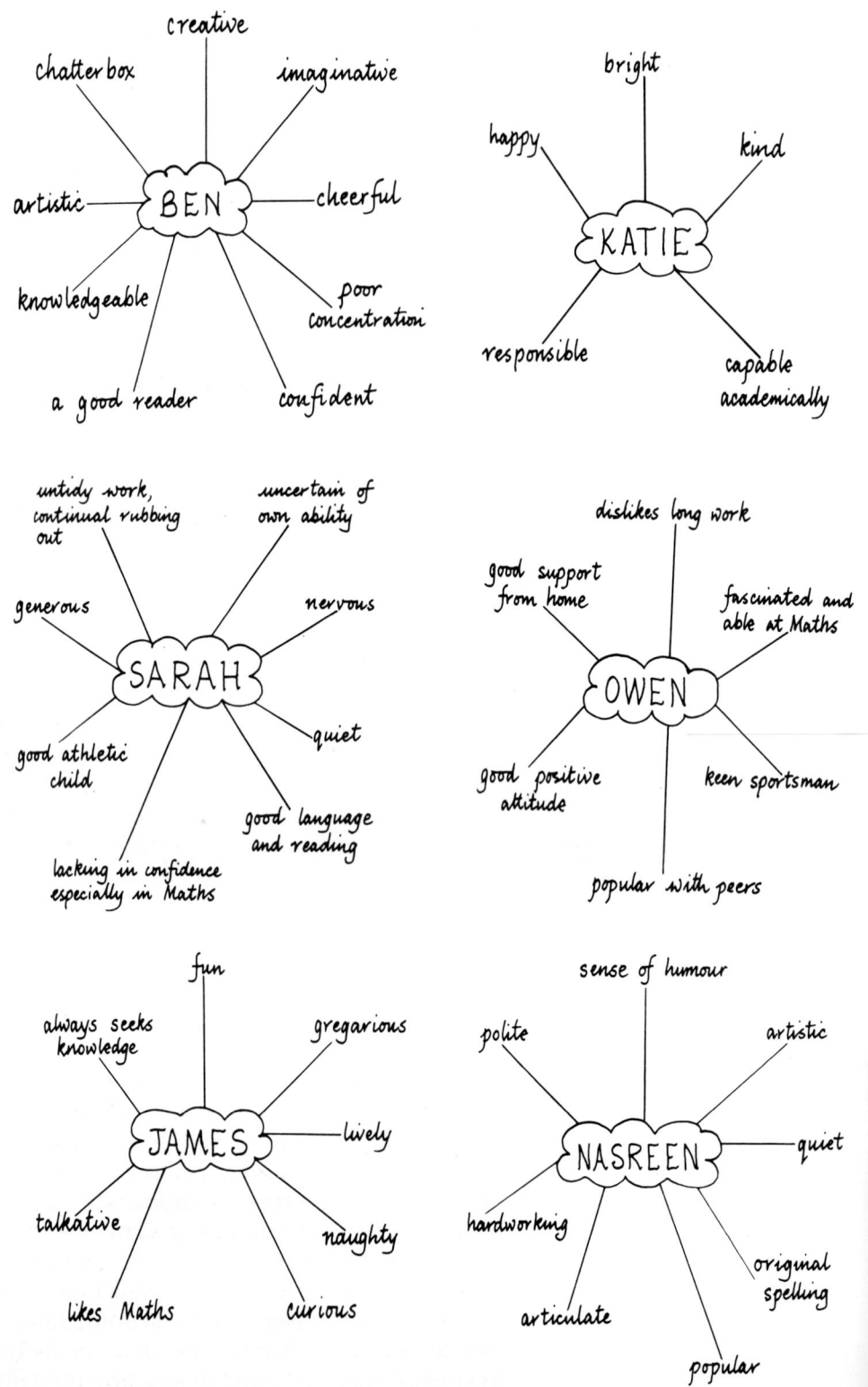

Ben: creative, chatter box, imaginative, artistic, cheerful, knowledgeable, poor concentration, a good reader, confident

Katie: bright, happy, kind, responsible, capable academically

Sarah: untidy work, continual rubbing out, uncertain of own ability, generous, nervous, quiet, good language and reading, lacking in confidence especially in Maths, good athletic child

Owen: dislikes long work, good support from home, fascinated and able at Maths, good positive attitude, keen sportsman, popular with peers

James: fun, always seeks knowledge, gregarious, lively, talkative, naughty, likes Maths, curious

Nasreen: sense of humour, polite, artistic, quiet, hardworking, original spelling, articulate, popular

Figure 3.1 *Snapshot descriptions*

extraordinarily complex. Neither does a greater focus upon intellectual development mean that the *process* elements of learning are sacrificed to *content* considerations. Rather, taking content and process together under the umbrella heading of 'intellectual development', the immediate need is to engage with the thorny problem of how to identify and describe children's learning in order to make possible the next stage of deciding how, and in which direction, to take the learning forward.

Beyond generalisations: establishing context

One way of beginning this process is to reflect upon some of the descriptions in Figure 3.1 and ask the question: 'What is meant by *"Ben is a good reader?"*' or, more precisely, 'What do *I* mean by *"Ben is a good reader?"*'

Do I mean he is fluent? reads silently? reads voraciously? reads with expression? uses phonic cues? Does he demonstrate *all* of these attributes on every occasion, or mainly fluency and use of phonic cues, with the rare appearance of expression? Similarly with James, who 'likes maths'. Delving a little deeper, does he like *all* of number (decimals, fractions, multiplication, division) as well as geometry, handling data, measurement and so on? What is the relationship between James' evident *liking* of mathematics and his *competence* in this area? Does one influence or cloud the vision of the other? In other words, is there an expectation that James not only likes mathematics but *can do* mathematics – whatever that might mean? And what of Owen who is 'fascinated and able in maths'? What does this mean to you? Or Sarah who is 'lacking in confidence, especially in maths'?

In order to begin to work on some of these questions and to unravel some of the complexities, it is helpful to look underneath or behind such generalisations as 'a good reader' or 'capable academically'. The first step is to detail the incident or incidents that gave rise to the generalisation in the first place. In other words, putting the generalisation into context enables both you and a wider audience to gain access to the thinking behind individual comments or assessments. The context clarifies what is meant by a 'good reader' *on this occasion*. At the same time, the context ensures a sense of perspective on the assessment procedure. You as the assessor are not claiming any more than that in this particular context, and at this particular moment in time, Ben is displaying certain of the qualities of good reader.

Towards shared meanings

Let us continue to explore the snapshot description in Figure 3.1. As you re-read the descriptions of the children, what pictures come to mind of the individual children? Physical attributes? Ponder for a while how far the physical appearance of a child influences your perception of their intellectual ability. Yet again, are you 'tougher' in your assessment of boys . . . or girls? No doubt some aspects of the images you begin to develop of Ben, Nasreen, James, Sarah, Katie and Owen will be shared by the teachers who wrote the original descriptions, but there will also be significant differences. There is no guarantee that the meaning assigned by one teacher to, for example, 'intelligent' matches the meaning assigned by another teacher. It is enlightening to fix upon individual words and to compare your own interpretation of meaning with a colleague. Is it possible to distinguish when you assign 'intelligent' as opposed to 'bright' as opposed to 'clever'? And what does 'laid back' mean to you? Confident? Lazy? Awkward? Extremely clever?

As you begin to explore meanings with colleagues it becomes clear once more that blanket expressions such as 'intelligent' are better defined in relation to individual learners and by providing the *context* within which the child can be described as 'intelligent'. It is necessary to acknowledge that we have to work towards a shared understanding and use of vocabulary. This involves sharing personal perspectives with colleagues, children and parents. Meanings can then be negotiated and renegotiated. This is not an instant, overnight business, but part of the ongoing, long-term staff and school development plan. Nevertheless it is something that, in a small way, you can begin tomorrow. As soon as you hear a colleague (or yourself) make a statement or generalisation, then ask for the context and begin to explore around and behind the words used! It's risky to expose your thinking in this way, but viewed as an essential part of professional development, it can be stimulating and well worth it in terms of classroom practice.

Negotiating agreement

The same process of negotiating and renegotiating meanings needs to be adopted when it comes to using the National Curriculum level descriptions as the criteria for assessing intellectual development. Part of the preparation for the Key Stage 1 Standard Assessment Tasks trials and pilot study (1990 and 1991) involved Y2 teachers in sharing their interpretations of the National Curriculum assessment requirements and working towards an agreed 'standard' interpretation based on examples of children's work that exemplified certain aspects of the attainment targets.

One of the positive features of the SATs pilot exercise work was the scope for Y2 teachers to meet together for discussion and support. All year-group teachers need to be involved in a similar process as part of developing a shared approach to teacher assessment. We are not suggesting that it is possible to ensure *complete* agreement of *all* teachers across the country on *all* level descriptions. That would be neither feasible nor desirable: professional debate is a vital ingredient of the assessment procedure and disagreement a healthy sign! Nevertheless, knowing more about how you and your colleagues view particular aspects and examples of children's work ensures a greater degree of consistency, which in turn contributes towards the overall coherence of the 'learning package' your school offers to its children and to the development of national standards of achievement. Chapter 9 provides one exercise (Inset Session 4) for sharing interpretations of level descriptions as part of school-based inservice work. The SCAA document *Children's Work Assessed* provides another starting point for work in this area.

Involving parents and children

At the same time as sharing perspectives with colleagues, there is scope to share with parents and children as well. Returning to the 'first thoughts' description of Figure 3.1, there is no means of knowing why Ben is assigned 'eloquent', James 'talkative', Nasreen 'articulate' without further dialogue. Inviting parents to provide information not necessarily available to you within the school setting adds another dimension, as does asking the children for their own perceptions or self-assessment. For example, it could be that James has little opportunity for talking at home as his three older brothers dominate the conversation, hence he is 'talkative' at school. Alternatively, he could be very anxious about his work at school, which would give a completely different insight into his running commentary in the classroom.

Nasreen and her 'original spelling' is an example of where a different kind of clarification is necessary. Asking the teacher who wrote this particular phrase for further clarification brought an unhesitating response from the other teachers in the group on her behalf: 'She *can't* spell!' It seems that in some instances, and for some teachers, being direct about children's achievement, or lack of it, is to be avoided. Inabilities are to be disguised by using ambiguous 'positive' phrases! So what is this all about? Pursuing this theme with one group of teachers revealed the influence of some past practice in report-writing, whereby teachers were required by headteachers to write only positive points. It seems there is a strong feeling amongst many teachers that some things just cannot be shared with parents or children. Yet teachers and parents share a common concern to ensure the best possible learning experiences for the children in their care. Giving meaningful feedback is part of the learning–assessing process and shares the responsibility between teachers, parents and children. Once perspectives are shared, then all parties can be involved in whatever next steps seem appropriate. Joint responsibility for building up a profile of an individual child provides the opportunity for maximum information to be available to teachers for planning the next learning experiences. At the same time, assessment is made more manageable and much less stressful. In the short term it takes time to establish workable routines and systems for involving parents and children, but the long-term benefits make it worthwhile. Undoubtedly, opening up more meaningful dialogue is a risky business. One way forward is to use the structure provided by the Formative Teacher Assessment Record described in Chapters 5 and 6 as a focus for discussion with parents and children.

Equal opportunities in assessment

A final look at the 'first thoughts' reveals:

```
          NASREEN
artistic
             hardworking
   quiet
             sensible
polite
       original spelling
```

```
              JAMES
likes maths         gregarious
   fun
              naughty    curious

   always seeks knowledge
```

```
┌─────────────────────────────┐   ┌──────────────────────────────┐
│           KATIE             │   │            OWEN              │
│                             │   │  fascinated and able at maths│
│    bright      happy        │   │                              │
│                             │   │     popular with peers       │
│                 kind        │   │                              │
│  responsible                │   │          keen sportsman      │
│                             │   │   good positive attitude     │
│   capable academically      │   │          dislikes long work  │
│                             │   │                              │
└─────────────────────────────┘   └──────────────────────────────┘
```

Listing and reviewing the vocabulary used in this exercise highlights gender and racial stereotypes and provides a challenging starting point for staff development. Invariably, in our experience of using this exercise with different groups of teachers, at least two-thirds of each group choose to focus on a boy. Whereas there *may* be very good reasons (purely coincidence?!) for this pattern to emerge with such predictable regularity, nevertheless it is interesting to ponder why (or indeed if) boys hold centre stage more often, and what the implications for girls and the assessment of girls might be. Again, sharing your own examples and incidents with colleagues can provide a useful forum for sharpening this particular debate. Just looking to see how many boys are considered to either 'like' or to be 'good' at maths is as good a starting point as any. Or look to see who are the scientists, or the fluent speakers, readers and writers. In this way, you can begin to explore some of your expectations of children which might influence your own assessment judgements.

In summary:
A number of working principles have emerged from the exercises and reflections in this chapter. There is a need to:

- ✦ attend to your personal concerns about assessment;
- ✦ identify how your past experiences of assessment influence you as an assessor now;
- ✦ move beyond personality to focus on intellectual development;
- ✦ move beyond generalisations and provide the context of the assessment;
- ✦ check and challenge your perceptions with:
  – colleagues,
  – children,
  – parents;

- move towards a shared vocabulary for describing what children can do;
- move towards some working definitions of the National Curriculum level descriptions;
- move towards a meaningful system of sharing the outcomes of assessment;
- consider equal opportunities in assessment.

4 The Planning–Learning–Assessing Cycle

In the previous chapter we used the 'first thoughts' exercise to start to generate a list of working principles for assessment. The list is incomplete and, like any set of working principles, is open both to challenge and to change. Our emphasis is on taking some time to develop a system of teacher assessment that is effective and manageable. This involves developing and refining principles and procedures along the way. *'But time is the one thing I don't have!'*, you cry in exasperation!

Very few people can cope instantly and successfully with juggling a whole range of new variables all at once. All the more reason then to build up new skills and procedures systematically. Gradually developing confidence in one new area in turn helps to shed some light on others. A prime example of this is record-keeping. *'What kind of records shall I keep?'* is a key concern for most teachers. Working parties develop a variety of highly commendable and beautifully produced documents. Teachers begin to assess the children and fill in the records. It is at this point that significant difficulties often emerge and the records are deemed 'unworkable', usually because they are too demanding in the amount of detail required. Developing records first and then fitting assessment around the records is not a helpful way of going about things. Instead, start by developing some assessment skills and a systematic approach to teacher assessment. In so doing, a workable record-keeping system will emerge, based upon classroom practice and experience. We focus on record-keeping in more detail in Chapter 9.

Sharing concerns: the why, who and what of assessment

'Where's the time for assessment coming from?' is a major concern and very real dilemma for many teachers but, in the same vein as record-keeping, is best resolved by first exploring:

- **Why** am I assessing?
- **Who** am I assessing?
- **What** am I assessing?

Why am I assessing?

> *One thing I'm looking forward to about assessment is ... being **required** to find out more about my children. I enjoy observing them but often feel under too much pressure (e.g. hearing them all read, keeping them all learning) to 'waste time' just watching.*
>
> (First school teacher)

One response to the question *'Why am I assessing?'* is a straightforward *'because there is a legal requirement to assess'*. So, how do you feel about being legally obliged to assess the children in your care? *'We're assessing all the time'* is a common response, often with the following rider: *'but why do we need to write it all down?'* Well, consider what happens when you are asked to write anything down. How does what you write compare with 'off the record' statements you might make about individual children?

Working on the 'Why?' query led us to review some of the official statements, for example:

> *The main objective of the assessment arrangements will be to ensure that each pupil's attainment in a subject and the elements within it can be clearly identified and the results used to help the pupil's progress. It is essential that the assessment arrangements establish what children know, understand and can do in order that teachers and parents can identify their children's strengths and weaknesses, and plan the next steps in their education.*
>
> (DES Circular 5/89, para. 41)

A common feature of many such statements is the link between assessing and planning. One way forward in the exploration of this link is to visualise an ongoing dynamic involving the teacher, the learner and something to be learned (Figure 4.1).

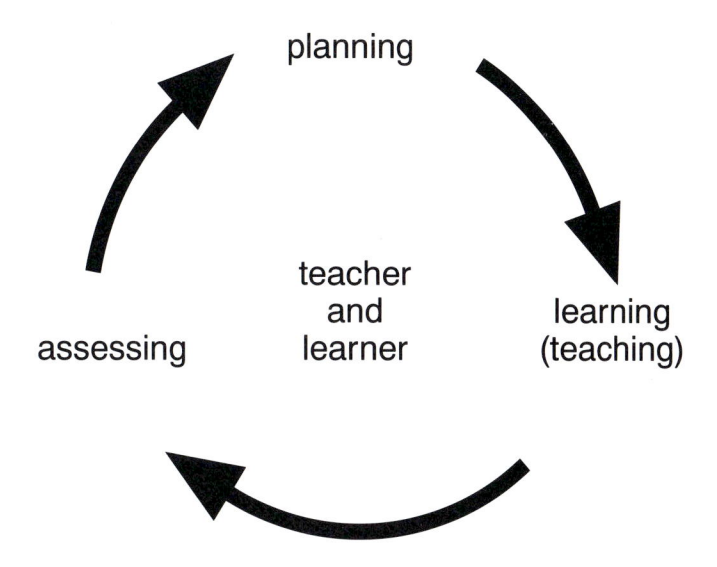

Figure 4.1 *The planning–learning–assessing dynamic*

Making each element of the dynamic distinct in this way reflects neither the reality of classroom life nor the complexity of learning and teaching, but needs to be seen as a starting point or device for thinking about assessment. At the moment, planning is undertaken with reference to the National Curriculum: learning experiences are planned using the appropriate documents as a guide to content. The current National Curriculum is of course only one of many possible ways of designing a curriculum and is itself subject to revision. But whereas, on the one hand, revision is a healthy sign that the curriculum debate continues, it's not always easy to respond positively to change when you are faced with revising your own planning and record-keeping. Planning activities to enable the learner to construct a route through the currculum is part of the teacher's role. Assessment provides feedback both to the learner and teacher as to how the journey is progressing, and provides the starting point for future planning. The planning–learning–assessing–planning dynamic continues. Wendy, a primary school teacher, comments:

❛ *It is only after a close assessment of what a child can do that future activities with any real progression can be identified and planned.* ❜

Getting to know individual children, and taking their learning forward accordingly, features strongly in the responses made by teachers when asked to complete the sentence '*One thing I'm looking forward to about assessment is . . .*'

'Getting a clearer picture of my pupils.'

'It will help to focus my attention more closely on the particular – both child and task.'

'Finding out new ways of exploring the development of an individual child.'

'Getting an "holistic" idea of the particular child.'

'I'll be able to watch children more closely.'

'To get to know them better and help them accordingly.'

The planning–learning–assessing relationship

Looking closely at individual children's learning provides you with information that can influence your next planning moves in a number of ways. Classroom life is full of conflicting needs and dilemmas. Part of your role as the teacher is to work with these conflicts and tensions. Amongst other things, this involves making decisions and choices about the learning experiences and resources available to the children at any particular moment in time. Making decisions and choices implies that you have something to base the decisions and choices upon, and this is where observations made during assessments of individual children play a key role.

One possible implication of this is that you should follow up each individual assessment by planning **individualised learning** packages. This may indeed by necessary on *some* occasions, but is not the only option available to you. How far individualised learning programmes are possible within any classroom depends on all kinds of other variables, including the number of children on roll, the range of resources available, teacher stamina and the children's autonomy: for many teachers the demands are unrealistic. There is also the broader issue as to how far individualised learning programmes are desirable and how far learning is enhanced, if not accelerated, by experience of collaborative working in groups.

The information gathered from individual assessments helps in deciding which learning 'packages' or activities to offer to which groups of children or individuals. Specific learning needs can be catered for within the same 'package'. For example, finding and recording the area of the classroom gives opportunity for Claire to practise measuring accurately, for Caroline to develop her recording skills and for Louise to work on addition of measurements. At the same time, all three will be involved in discussing, decision-making, cooperating, using calculators and so on.

Authentic activity

Choosing or designing tasks that are rich in their potential for supporting children's learning across a range of skills and knowledge is part and parcel of the everyday practice of teaching. It is an essential strategy for busy teachers faced with the increased content demands of the National Curriculum and large classes of children. At the same time, if the starting point given to children is rich enough in possible learning outcomes, then it will in turn provide an excellent focus for assessment purposes.

In other words, there is no *need* to design special assessment tasks (mini-SATs) in order to carry out teacher assessments.

Identifying the kind of task that is suitable for assessment purposes is a cause for anxiety amongst many teachers. For some, assessment activities are somehow different to learning activities and need to be specially thought out or specially devised. This is indeed how much of the assessment work both past and present has been carried out. Up until now there has been a marked tendency to leave assessment until the end of a period of time or until the end of the topic being studied. Tests, exams or some other assessment activity is then administered and results noted, often for summative and discriminatory (allocation of scarce resources) purposes only. The grip that this approach to assessment has on all of us is hard to shake!

The planning–learning–assessing model re-focuses attention on the formative aspects of assessment and highlights the positive contributions teacher assessment can make to the teaching–learning dynamic. This is no easy task, given the formal procedures of reporting SAT results with TA at the end of Key Stages. Naturally enough, these summative requirements weigh heavily, particularly for Y2 and Y6 teachers. However, giving the formative dimension high priority not only informs your daily practice and enhances children's learning, but also generates the information you need to complete summative records as and when required. Working on assessment the other way round – that is, giving priority to devising tasks and tests to ensure that you have accurate summative information – provides limited feedback in terms of daily classroom practice relative to the amount of energy and time given to devising the tests and tasks in the first instance! For the most part, tests and special assessment tasks are best left to outside agencies who have the time to devise them. In other words, the planning–learning–assessing framework favours Approach A in Figure 4.2, whilst recognising that Approach B is a strategy that may be called upon in particular cases.

Approach A

planning → learning activities → assessing → (back to learning activities)

Approach B

planning → learning activities; planning → assessing activities

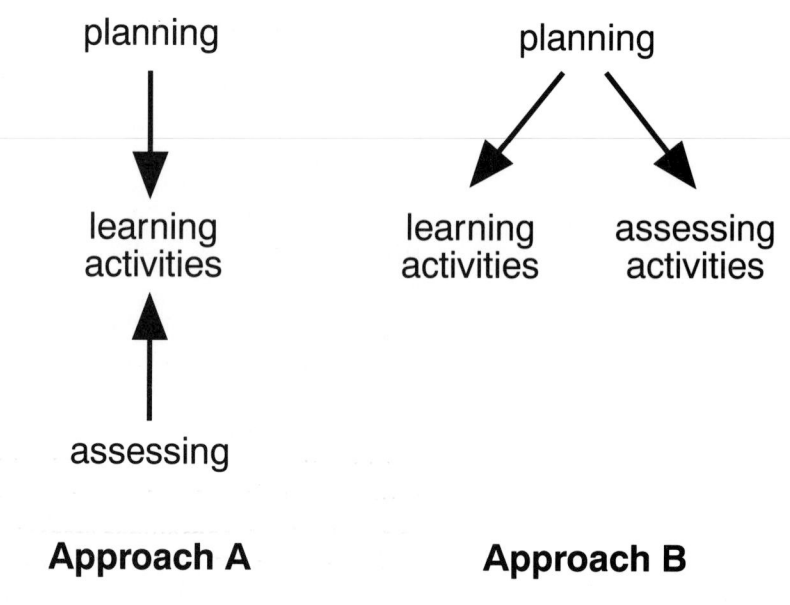

Figure 4.2 *Two strategies for planning and assessing*

What am I assessing?

> *Teacher Assessment is the continuing process of judging individual children's work.*
>
> (SCAA School Assessment Folder)

Exploring the 'Why?' of assessment, above, resulted in links being made between assessment informing the planning of learning activities, and the learning activities themselves providing the focus for assessment. In this way, part of the answer to the question *'What am I assessing?'* has already been uncovered: children's responses to learning activities or, put more simply, children's learning.

Of course, in order to make sense of what this means in practice, it is necessary to pursue the theme a little further. One of the most significant differences between past assessment practices and current orthodoxy is the emphasis upon **positive achievement** – the focus on what children *know, understand and can do*. Past practice has invariably favoured a deficit model, by highlighting what children are *unable* to do and leaving implicit what they can do! Changing this approach takes time and practice, but there are considerable benefits, as described by primary teacher, Wendy:

> *Trying to restrict myself to only positive comments . . . is a valuable exercise. It made me realise how much a child can do and I found myself thinking more positively about that child's abilities.*

Wendy found herself 'thinking more positively' about the abilities of individual children. Teacher expectation is a powerful thing. If the focus of attention is predominantly on children's *in*abilities, then this is bound to influence the image held by the teacher of individual learners. This in turn will influence the kinds of learning activities that are offered to individuals. A somewhat stereotypical example would be preventing children who have some difficulty with standard algorithms in mathematics from engaging with more challenging investigational work. Pages of routine sum practice are offered instead.

Take five minutes to try this exercise, preferably with a colleague. Close your eyes and let your mind wander amongst the children in your class. Choose any two children. Make a list of what immediately springs to mind as to what each child *is* able to do, and then list some of the things each child is *not* able to do. Don't agonise – make some immediate responses. What do you notice about the lists?

Consider the implications of taking what the learner *is able to do* as your starting point for planning future activities. Planning in such a way challenges the more usual practice of 'plugging gaps' – that is, designing specific tasks to 'help' the learner with what he/she *cannot* do. What is the potential for starting from developing strengths? Try both approaches and discuss with colleagues the differences.

Sampling aspects of children's learning

One of the guiding principles for assessment that emerged from the 'first thoughts' exercise in Chapter 3 was the need to pay more attention to the intellectual development of children: to move beyond personality. Getting to know the intellectual dimension of children involves looking at the outward manifestations of their learning and giving the best possible interpretation of what you perceive. In essence, you can look at:

✦ what the child **does** (action);
✦ what the child **says**;
✦ what the child **puts down on paper** (writing, drawing, making).

Any one of the above can be looked at in isolation, or in any combination of two out of three, or all three together. As with any analysis, on paper it all seems very neat and straightforward – no problem! But classroom life is far less tidy, far more exciting and messy. One immediate dilemma you will be faced with is which option or combination to choose. *'I might miss the vital clue if I only focus on one or other'*, you might say. In which case, going for all three to ensure optimum information every time may in fact feel like the only real option available to you. Not at all. Another, more pragmatic approach involves making the best possible use of *whatever* data you have available to you at any particular moment in time, at the same time recognising both the potential and necessary limitations of both the data and the assessment based upon that data.

Most teachers are concerned to provide the best possible opportunities for each child to demonstrate what they know, understand and can do. As Angela writes:

❛ *The worry is that what we choose to observe and how we choose to do it will affect what we find. If assessment is not organised carefully and accurately enough, then the children won't be able to demonstrate what they know and understand.* **9**

This whole area touches upon some very real anxieties. Many of the teachers' responses to completing the 'one thing I'm worried about assessment is . . .' sentence centred upon:

+ being fair,
+ getting a true picture,
+ being accurate.

If these concerns are juxtaposed with the day-to-day management of the classroom as a learning environment, it is easy to see why they weigh heavily. The conflicting demands of classroom life make the whole business of making assessments seem impossible – no wonder anxiety levels rise! This is where it is important to set some workable boundaries that will help to resolve, but not altogether remove, the conflicts. Try taking a fresh look at the expectations you have of yourself within the assessment context. Assuming that you share the expectations underlying the worries above, try revisiting them in the following way:

+ being fair *enough*,
+ getting a true *enough* picture,
+ being accurate *enough*.

In other words, instead of trying to provide the *perfect* assessment (and learning environment), go for assessment (and a learning environment) that is *good enough*. In effect this means ceasing to strive for the perfect assessment task, the perfect assessment environment, the perfect moment for assessment, but instead getting on with assessment in the here and now of your busy classroom and recognising it for what it is.

This links back with the importance of giving the *context* of the assessment, as raised in Chapter 3. You give your best shot at assessing whatever is available to you at particular moments in time and within particular contexts: no more, no less. Adopting this approach ensures you have some energy left to make effective *use* of your teacher assessment.

The context, and the nature of the activity the children are working on, will also help you to decide whether to assess a piece of written work, or what the learner says or does, or any of the combinations in between. Some activities do not have any written outcomes; others are primarily concerned with putting something on paper. Of course, assessing a piece of recording does not preclude asking the learner to talk about the piece of work as well, but you will need to consider whether asking the child to talk about the work as well is a workable option, given the everyday constraints of classroom life. Listening to what the learner says can itself take place in a number of ways:

- child and one other child,
- child and teacher,
- child in small group,
- child reporting back to large or whole class.

Who am I assessing?

At first sight there doesn't seem to be much of a problem with answering the question *'Who am I assessing?'* All the children in your care need to be part of your ongoing teacher assessment programme. Digging a little deeper, however, there are a number of questions lurking behind the original:

- how many children at any one time?
- should the children be grouped?
- what kind of groupings are best?
- how often?

In many ways you are spoilt for choice in these areas, as the possible combinations and permutations are many and various. One deciding factor will be whether a specific option works for you in your classroom and within your school. Different approaches will work best at different times and continue to evolve and develop with experience. Faced with so much choice, and coupled with the anxieties of getting it 'right' or 'perfect', it's easy enough to see why it's hard to begin! Nevertheless, it's all a bit like learning to swim: once you've dipped your toe in the water, it can only get better.

One key to getting started is to keep in mind the principle that teacher assessment is linked to the day-to-day teaching and learning process. In which case, you can make a start by looking at the daily routine for, say, tomorrow, and decide which part of the day provides you with a fairly accessible assessment opportunity:

	9.00	10.45	12.00	1.45	3.00	
TUESDAY	Maths	Topic		Assembly	Swimming	Story

The slot between 10.45 and 12.00 seems quite hopeful. Review the plans you have made for the topic work. Choose one of the activities that the children will be working on at that time and identify four children for you to assess. Of course it's possible that all the children in your class are pursuing their own line of enquiry within the topic, in which case you might need to focus on:

✦ Four children, working *individually* on *different* tasks and probably located in *different* parts of the classroom (Figure 4.3).

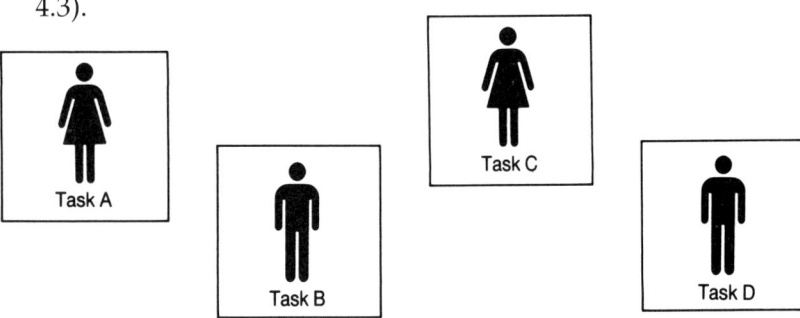

Figure 4.3 *Children working individually on **different** tasks*

In terms of the swimming metaphor introduced earlier, this scenario is equivalent to diving from the high board and completing a triple loop somersault on your first swimming lesson – possible, but not to be recommended!

Something a little more manageable would be either:

✦ Four children working *individually* on the *same* task and located in the same place (Figure 4.4), or

Figure 4.4 *Children working individually on the **same** task*

✦ Four children working *collaboratively* on the same task located in the same place (Figure 4.5).

Figure 4.5 *Children working **collaboratively** on the same task*

Initially, option 2 is the most straightforward and least problematic way to begin developing an assessment procedure.

Who you choose to assess at any particular moment is inextricably linked with how you choose to manage and organise your classroom as a learning environment: the kinds of tasks you offer and how, and whether you group children. Different aspects of classroom management and organisation are illustrated and discussed in Chapter 7. For the moment, get started on teacher assessment by working within the framework of your everyday classroom practice or, at the very most, with minimal adjustments to normal routines. These initial experiences can be used to inform any longer-term changes that you may wish to make.

Four is a good number

For most assessment purposes, and for the approach suggested in the next chapter, four children seems to be a comfortable number to cope with, either at any one time or during any one day. Any more than four and it becomes difficult for you to manage the amount of information available to you from each child. Any less than four and it becomes difficult to manage to assess the whole class on a regular basis. Remember: you can always vary the approach according to particular circumstances, but four a day is something to have in mind.

Another challenging question seems to be *'How often?'*. Staying with the principle that effective teacher assessment is part and parcel of the daily planning–learning–assessing routine, then opportunities for assessment during learning activities should be available on a daily basis. Whether it is possible for you to *make use* of each assessment opportunity will depend on the other demands and priorities of particular days. Clearly, there are days where your attention may be predominantly focused elsewhere – for example, rehearsal days for special festivals, parent assembly days, book week, visits by community police, to name but a few. Similarly, there will be unexpected disruptions on some days, or you will be engaged for longer than anticipated with one group of children on a particular activity. Reviewing assessment plans will feature as part of your daily review of learning. As you reconsider the learning experiences you are planning to offer tomorrow in the light of what the children actually did today, then it follows that some rescheduling or shifting of the focus for assessment may occur. Nevertheless, it *is* possible to give yourself a basic assessment framework or routine.

Getting the habit

'I know I just need to develop the habit' is how deputy head, Kate, expressed her stance to the National Curriculum assessment requirements. Adopting a fairly mechanical, pragmatic approach helps to get the ball rolling in the first instance. Begin by developing the idea raised on page 42 and review your daily routines to identify possible assessment opportunities throughout the week. Highlight the time slots on your timetable and share the information with other colleagues as well as the children in your class. If others know of your plans, then they can begin to take some responsibility for supporting you (e.g. endeavouring not to interrupt you for short periods of time).

Giving yourself one day in the week where you are free from assessing in any systematic or formal way should still enable you to assess a class of 32 children over a two-week cycle: 4 children a day across 8 out of 10 days = 32 children assessed.

It follows from the planning–learning–assessing principle that the children will be assessed during the learning activity they are working on for that day. This means that not all the children will necessarily be assessed on the *same* activities during the two-week assessment cycle. Assessing children on the same activity falls within the province of SATs and assessment for summative purposes. Effective *teacher assessment* is primarily concerned with formative purposes – building up a profile of supporting individual learning over a period of time – and so it is perfectly acceptable to complete assessments during different activities for different groups of children.

Having completed one assessment cycle across the two weeks (it may take three weeks to complete a cycle sometimes), then the order for assessing children can be changed and new

46 EFFECTIVE TEACHER ASSESSMENT

			9 am	10.30–10.45	Infs: 11.45–1.15 Jnrs: 12.15–1.15	Year 4	2.30–2.45	3.30
MONDAY	QUIET READING TIME 9am UNTIL 9.30am	ASSEMBLY APPROX. 9.45am UNTIL 9.30am	Spelling News	Maths	Topic		Handwriting	
TUESDAY			Maths	PE (middle hall)	Look and Read TV video and Worksheet	2.10 Singing	DRAMA Finish Look and Read	↑ Story ↓
WEDNESDAY			Games	Maths Language	Science (practical work) Mrs Bailey →		Mrs D → GYM	
THURSDAY	EVERY MORNING FROM 9am	EVERY MORNING FROM 9.30am	Maths	Swimming	11.45 Singing	Handwriting	Language Topic work	
FRIDAY			Mrs Shaheed Language Fortnightly Library visit	Maths	Spelling Test	Craft afternoon Mrs Raynsford Mrs Bailey Mrs Simpson Mrs Hussain		

Figure 4.6 Timetable highlighted for assessment opportunities

groupings formed, if appropriate for the next cycle. Offering neat solutions is pretty straightforward on paper but classroom life is much less clearly defined! Nevertheless, establishing a *routine* for looking at children's learning in a structured way is an essential part of effective teacher assessment. Following the two-week cycle plan enables you to get started and provides a framework which you can adapt to suit your individual circumstance. This whole approach enables you to look closely at children's learning on a sampling basis, which in turn enables you to build up a profile of attainment throughout the Key Stage.

Action Plan reminders

+ Look at the programme or timetable for learning across the next two weeks. Identify assessment opportunities, especially times when other adult support is available.
+ List which children will be assessed on which days and on which activities during the first two-week cycle.
+ Share your plans with children and colleagues and enlist their support. Establish some rules to enable you to spend *short* intervals of time observing and assessing.

5 Teacher Assessment in Action: looking at children's learning

In the previous two chapters we have rehearsed some of the anxieties and dilemmas surrounding an initial foray into the world of assessment. The prime focus of this chapter is to outline and follow through one approach to teacher assessment based on looking at children's learning and with the planning–learning–assessing cycle and formative aspects of assessment firmly in mind.

Taking the plunge!

By now you will have identified for yourself some slots during your weekly routine when you could assess four children. Let's suppose you have chosen the time and identified the particular learning activity that the children will be working on at that time. On this occasion the children will be working individually but on the same task – alternative options are outlined on pages 43–4. The next decision to be taken is whether to sit with the children for a short period of time, or whether to return to the group at regular intervals. Each option has its advantages and disadvantages.

Sitting with the group for a short period of time is helpful in terms of providing you with the opportunity to focus on the task in hand in a sustained and concentrated way. One disadvantage of this approach voiced by many teachers is *'What are the rest of the class doing while I'm sitting with a small group?'* Well, spend five minutes reviewing your normal classroom practice and identify the times when you already give your attention to a small group only – what are the rest of the class doing at those times? Perhaps equally important at this juncture is to clarify what we mean by sitting with a small group, in terms of length of time. In Chapter 4 we talked of assessments being fair *enough*, accurate *enough*, true *enough*. This involves making the best possible use of the data or information available to you at particular moments in time and not placing impossible demands upon yourself to collect more and more just in case you miss the vital clue.

On rare occasions, then, it might be possible to sit with the group for the duration of a task, but this is certainly not a necessary condition for effective assessment to take place. The *analysis* of your observations is the vital ingredient. Capturing one small incident from the activity of an individual learner can speak volumes. As primary teacher Denise comments:

> *I found that I did not have to stay very long with the children before I had plenty of material to work on. I just watched them for about five minutes and jotted down what they did. . . .*

Returning to a group of children at regular intervals has the advantage of allowing you to sample a variety of the children's responses to the activity, but is a more difficult strategy to employ initially – in terms of requiring you to move in and out of close observation 'mode' and handle all the other queries that might be coming your way from the children you are not assessing at that moment. Beginning with a five-minute observation time sitting with the group is as good a way in as any. It's handy to have a notebook on the first few occasions you try some close observation work, although at a later date you may feel confident enough to fill in the 'account' section of the Formative Teacher Assessment Record (Figure 5.1) actually during the observation time.

The format for this Record evolved in response to the question *'How do I make the move from observing to assessing?'* The Record offers a minimal framework that can be redesigned to accommodate individual preferences in the light of professional experience. Although the prime purpose of the Record is to provide a structure to support effective teacher assessment, at the same time we suggest it becomes an integral feature of your record-keeping system. Chapter 9 develops the theme of how the Formative Teacher Assessment Record based on close observation can form a central part of your record-keeping package.

Exploring the Formative Teacher Assessment Record

The Formative Teacher Assessment Record reflects the planning–learning–assessing dynamic considered earlier. Each

| FORMATIVE TEACHER ASSESSMENT RECORD | Y1 ☐ Y2 ☐ Y3 ☐ |
| | Y4 ☐ Y5 ☐ Y6 ☐ |

Name : .... Date : ....

Activity : ....

Possible Outcomes

Account	Interpretation	Action

Comments :

Figure 5.1 *The Formative Teacher Assessment Record*

The authors and publishers grant permission for copies of this Record to be made for classroom and inset purposes.

section helps to inform the next until the 'Action' column, which in turn can help to define the next planning moves, i.e. the next 'Possible Outcomes'.

Possible Outcomes		
why have I planned this activity?		
Account	**Interpretation**	**Action**
what actually happened? *what did the child do, say, write or make?*	*what does this tell me about the learner?* *what does the child know, understand or do?*	*how does this help my next planning?* *what might I plan next?*

Comments :

any additional comments from the teacher, child or parents

Figure 5.2 *The planning–learning–assessing–planning dynamic reflected in the Record*

There is space to record the usual details of the name of the child observed and assessed, and the date of the observation and assessment. In addition, there is space to outline the nature of the activity that the children are working on. This ensures that the assessment is seen for what it is: an assessment at a particular moment in time and embedded in a particular context. The format includes a 'Comments' section which can be used by the teacher, child or parent to record additional information or responses to the particular observation and assessment.

Identifying 'Possible Outcomes'

A major part of your role as a teacher involves planning learning experiences or activities for the children in your care. Different activities encapsulate different learning experiences, and you choose to offer a particular activity to a particular group of children because of its potential in terms of learning outcomes. In other words, you hope that the children will learn certain things by engaging with the activity. As active participants in their own learning, children will bring something of themselves to the activity and so there is no guarantee that they will learn all or even part of what you had intended. They may branch off in an equally valid and productive direction. So much the better. Nevertheless, the purpose of this column is to record the *possible* learning outcomes of the activity that you are observing and assessing the children working on. It is helpful to identify the possible learning outcomes in this way, as they will provide prompts as to what to look out for during the observation and assessment. At the same time, it's as well not to develop tunnel vision by being so busy looking for the *possible outcomes* during your observation time that you miss the *actual outcomes* – and by implication you miss the opportunity to complete assessments on other than the possible outcomes!

Considering 'Possible Outcomes' can be quite an eye-opener, as Barbara describes:

❛ *These sheets force me to review the range of tasks that I give to the children. In order to list the possible outcomes I have to be specific about* ***why*** *I am giving a particular activity. Is the child actually learning much from it intellectually? It is sometimes too easy to put out an activity and be very woolly about what the child is meant to be doing, apart from learning socialisation skills, or worse still, 'learning independence'. Both these skills are commendable in their own right but are attainable through most tasks. To assess [and develop] a child's intellectual development, much more specific activities must be selected.* ❜

Why this activity?

'Possible Outcomes' centres on the *learning* potential of an activity or task and answers the question *'Why have I planned to use this task?'*. In other words you are identifying and making a note of your aims or rationale for offering particular activities to the children. In this way, 'Possible Outcomes' links with good planning practice and is not something 'extra' you have to do for assessment purposes. The assessment possibilities from any one activity follow on from having identified the learning possibilities.

The crucial missing ingredient in all this so far is of course **the learner**! How each learner responds to the task will determine the actual learning, and therefore the assessment outcomes. Each response provides you with something to assess, and contributes to the profile that you and your colleagues are building up of individual children throughout each Key Stage. It's important to keep the idea of building up a profile in mind for teacher assessment, because there will be times when the child you are observing behaves in what you consider to be a very untypical way. Now, if this were the *only* opportunity you were going to have to assess the child, then you would quite rightly feel concerned that the picture you were getting was not a sufficiently fair one. However, teacher assessment is part of your weekly routine, and so there will be other opportunities – in different contexts and possibly with a different teacher – for the child to demonstrate different attainments. Sharing with the children the fact that you are looking closely at what they are doing that day, in order to assess them, will encourage the children to show what they can do, although, inevitably, there will always be some for whom that day is not a good day, for whatever reason! Developing an ethos in your classroom whereby assessment is a *shared responsibility* is something worth working towards.

Giving an 'Account'

The 'Account' section is where you report your observations of how the child responded to the task or activity. This is not as easy as it sounds, and needs practice! Angela describes her experience:

❢ *The observation – that is 'account' – needs skill in recording exactly what is seen and heard without value judgements being made. In this section I found I had added value judgements – for example 'unable to' – instead of either not writing anything or recording the answer to my question 'Why do you think . . .?, even if the answer was non-verbal, such as a shrug of the shoulders.* **❯**

Giving an account involves relating what you *actually noticed and heard* as the children worked on the activity.

It's helpful to use a separate notebook on your first few observations and to scribble down more or less everything. The process of translating your notes to the 'Account' section of the Formative Teacher Assessment Record will help you to keep a check on whether you are sticking to giving an account or whether some of your own thoughts and assumptions are beginning to appear. As you practise observing and recording in this way, you will become more adept at writing succinct notes which will provide you with enough information to make some meaningful assessments *and* remain manageable within the classroom context. Sharing your first few attempts with a colleague is risky but will provide you with useful feedback. Some completed examples of Formative Teacher Assessment Records are explored later in Chapter 6 and other examples are included in the Appendix, but nothing compares with doing some for yourself and sharing the experience with colleagues.

Before you complete your first close observation in the classroom, you might like to watch a short video extract of children working on an activity. Make your own observation notes and then compare your observations with a colleague. Devise an 'account' together for one or more of the children you observed. As you become more practised at saying what you see and noting what you hear, you will become more selective and more naturally focus on the aspects of what the children are doing that link most directly with their learning development.

Making an 'Interpretation'

The observations that you have give in the 'Account' section of the Record now become the focus for interpretation, assessment and action. Revisit the 'account' with the following questions in mind: *'What does this account tell me about the learner? In particular, what does it tell me about what she/he knows, understands and is able to do?'* Some people prefer to use the word 'judgment' here rather than 'interpretation' – that's fine. We use the word 'interpretation' as a reminder of the complexity of assessing children's learning. Whatever is recorded in this column is your 'best shot' according to the data available and with all the necessary limitations of the particular context.

Once again, the theory of how to fill in this section of the assessment record is easily put down on paper but not so easy to put into practice. Many teachers at first found it extremely hard to identity what it was that children knew or understood or were able to do. Saying what children *cannot* do seems to come more naturally. However, with a little perseverance it is possible to begin to identify a range of attainments from one account and subsequently make connections with the National Curriculum attainment targets.

Pat comments:

*I found the interpretation a little difficult at first as I saw what they had **not** achieved. When I started to be more positive this section became easier. I found that they knew more than I thought.*

And Barbara:

It is the interpretation of the work done on the task that one can appropriately refer to the National Curriculum. . . . One of the hardest things when considering the completion of this column is to keep one's comments positive. Remarks such as 'he was not very systematic' should instead be turned into positive future plans and entered in the 'Action' column.

Deciding upon 'Action'

'Action' was the most useful part of the sheet for me as I could see what I needed to do in the future.

(Primary school teacher)

Effective teacher assessment not only involves looking closely at children's learning and offering some interpretations, but also moving to the next stage – of making use of the information gathered to plan subsequent learning experiences. In this way, the 'Action' section of the Formative Teacher Assessment Record completes the assessment cycle by taking you back to the planning stage of the planning–learning–assessing dynamic. This relationship with everyday practice is one of the distinguishing features of formative teacher assessment: there's something tangible in it for both you and the children.

As Wendy comments:

> *Being asked to be specific about future action was valuable for me. I feel I too often think in vague terms about where a child needs to go next. This served to highlight very specific areas and not necessarily of an academic nature, e.g. would Veronica perform equally as well with a more dominant partner? Since she always chooses to work with two other rather 'retiring' girls, I have never observed her closely in a different situation. She pleasantly surprised me by her capable solution and logical method of working and I would now like to see her facing more challenging problems of this nature.*

Wendy's observations of Veronica have prompted her not only to consider 'what next?' for Veronica in terms of more challenging content, but also 'what next?' in terms of working partners for Veronica. In other words, the close observation has provided some insight into how Wendy might choose to regroup some of her children on a future occasion to enhance and support learning. Observations of other children will provide similar insights which can then be used to review how you organise and manage the classroom as a learning environment.

Making choices

Often, one observation will provide a long list of possibilities for the 'Action' section and this can be a little daunting, to say the least! Sometimes it will only be possible to follow through one or two 'actions' in the immediate future; sometimes the only action you take is *not* to take action on that occasion, and sometimes the action you take is at a tangent to the actual action listed.

Using the Record to involve children and parents

The approach to teacher assessment described so far may have somewhat given the impression that assessment is something done by you to the children. Undoubtedly, in the first instance it is sensible to focus upon yourself and your own role and developing skills. Once you feel more confident about the whole process – in other words, once you have begun to shape your own story about assessment – then the Formative Teacher Assessment Record can be used to enlarge the circle of participants involved in the assessment. This can happen in a number of ways and the options need to be explored over a significant period of time as part of the school development work on assessment.

At one level you can read the 'Account' and 'Interpretation' sections of the Record to the child and note her or his response in the 'Comments' section. You may in fact want to add some additional comments of your own in this section, if you feel there is something to say about this particular close observation and assessment that has not already been recorded in any of the other columns. Asking parents to comment is also a possibility at this stage, although you will need to think creatively about whether to develop a system of:

- sending the Records home for comments as and when they are completed; or
- having the Records available in school for parents to comment on at regular intervals; or
- using the Records to focus discussion on parents' afternoons or evenings.

Choosing to share your observations provides the opportunity for parents to become familiar with the kinds of activities and learning experiences on offer in your classroom. The Formative Teacher Assessment Records give highly specific samples of children's experiences at school and highlight individual progress. There is something very concrete for all the concerned parties to work on! Demystifying classroom life enables parents to provide purposeful support to your work of enabling children to learn. Using the Record to focus attention, parents can:

- provide you with additional information as to what children know, understand and can do;
- provide support at home for the areas identified in the 'Action' section.

Using the Formative Teacher Assessment Record as part of a recording and reporting system and as an integral part of a Record of Achievement is discussed in Chapter 8.

Developing children's self-assessment by conferencing

At another level, the children's own involvement and skills of **self-assessment** can be developed not just by using the Formative Teacher Assessment Record process and format, but by sharing with the children some of the principles behind meaningful self-assessment. In many instances, self-assessments suffer from generalisations along the same lines as the 'first thoughts' exercise in Chapter 3. Often the focus centres on whether the child *enjoyed* the activity or not, which, although important, often leaves very little, if any, space for comments on actual achievement or recommendations for future learning programmes. Some examples of children's self-assessment reports are included in Chapter 8 (Figure 8.3 illustrates a self-assessment that includes future action: 'things to remember for the future').

Using the Formative Teacher Assessment Record as part of a *conferencing* system with children can provide a way into encouraging children to be more specific in their self-assessments and subsequently taking some responsibility for the next steps in their learning. 'Conferencing' can take a variety of forms and can involve:

- child – teacher
- small group of children – teacher
- child – teacher – parents

An essential feature of any conference is to provide a forum for sharing information. The individual sections of the Formative Teacher Assessment Record help to focus attention on *highly specific* and *manageable amounts* of information. Some of the advantages of sharing this information with the children during classroom-based conferences can be highlighted by revisiting each section of the Record.

Reading the 'Account' section together with the child puts the child in the picture as to what you actually observed him or her doing. Many teachers have mused with us as to whether they should let the children know that they are being observed and assessed. There is a concern that the children will feel 'under pressure'. Feeling 'under pressure' is probably something we have all felt at some time or another within the realm of summative assessments – piano/music exams, GCEs/GCSEs, A Levels, degree exams, and so on. Teacher assessment as part of the ongoing planning–learning–assessing dynamic has a different focus, and as part of the everyday learning experience is supported by the classroom ethos that you have already established. Children need to be clear that monitoring their progress is part of your job! The 'Account' section of the Record gives a very immediate kind of feedback to the children on what you have noticed about them on one occasion. They might also be able to add to the account something you have missed.

As you move on to share the 'Interpretation' section with the children, you can highlight where your interpretations relate back to your observations in the 'Account'. In this way, you can begin to discuss with children how your assessments are based upon what they do, say or put down on paper (plus combinations in between) and so the more they can share with you the better. At the same time, you can use the 'Interpretation' section to illustrate that you are looking out for what they can do, what they do know and what they do understand. Looking at a number of Formative Teacher Assessment Records together over a period of time helps to build up a picture of positive attainment and enhances self-esteem.

Again, it's possible that during the discussion the children will identify and demonstrate to you small but significant extensions to the list of 'Interpretations'. Giving children insight into how you assess enables them to make connections and to develop their own skills at self-assessment which in turn can move full circle and make a contribution to your own assessments.

Taking children through the 'Action' suggestions provides them with some concrete next steps in their learning. It is possible for you to be so caught up in the planning and preparation of activities for a whole class of children that you forget to share with them the purpose behind the activities they are working on. The National Curriculum provides a framework for your own planning and could usefully be shared with the children. Giving children some idea of what they need to attend to next gives a sense of direction to what they are doing, and also increases their awareness of what you will be looking out for in terms of future assessments – both yours and their own self-assessments. Sharing the Formative Teacher Assessment Records in this way provides some very clear boundaries for the children in terms of your expectations. You can isolate particular aspects of individual performance and follow them through either with the individual concerned or with a small group of children or the whole class.

Keeping a sense of perspective

At this point you may be feeling that familiar rising sense of panic as to where you will find the time for this kind of conference exchange, in amongst the myriad other requirements of classroom life. Let's try to put the whole procedure into a working perspective, firstly by acknowledging that it probably takes longer to write and read about such a process than it does to actually carry out a conference! Secondly, if conferencing is not part of your current practice, then view it as a second or third stage in your development of a systematic approach to teacher assessment and don't feel you have to take on board a whole set of new practices until you are ready. Once you feel more comfortable with completing the Formative Teacher Assessment Record by looking closely at children's learning, then gradually involving children more and more in the whole process will seem like a natural next step. Thirdly, the time taken to complete the close observation and conferencing cycle in the short term creates time in the long term, as children have a clearer sense of direction as to where they are heading in their learning and can be trained to take greater responsibility for their own learning. Once again, this is not an overnight happening and benefits from being a whole-school approach reflected in school policies. Finally, the model of teacher assessment reflected in the structure of the Formative Teacher Assessment Record is based upon a *sampling* procedure carried out over *at least* a two-week period. Not *every* learning experience that the children work through will be part of the close observation–assessment–conference cycle: just enough to provide a significant but manageable amount of data for all concerned.

6 Using the Formative Teacher Assessment Record

In this chapter we take a closer look at some completed Records to see how the theory outlined in Chapter 5 actually works in practice! Initially, the focus will be on examples of assessments that have taken place during mathematics lessons. Looking at assessments from a single subject area is simply a device to illustrate as clearly as possible some of the points you need to bear in mind as you begin to use the assessment format for yourself. Starting your own observations by looking at an activity from one subject area only is a good idea, in that it gives you a chance to 'contain' the whole procedure in a manageable way. But by now you will have picked up our theme of using your first experiences to inform your next; moving from observing single-subject tasks to tasks that incorporate a number of subject areas is an excellent case in point. Further examples of completed Formative Teacher Assessment Records from different areas are included in the Appendix.

So far, we have established teacher assessment as part of an ongoing planning–learning–assessing dynamic in which the link between assessment and deciding on the next learning experiences is of paramount importance. A systematic sampling procedure of looking closely at children's learning is supported by using a structured Formative Teacher Assessment Record. An essential feature of this approach is the relationship between each step in the assessment cycle, reflected in each section of the record format. 'Possible Outcomes' are kept in the back of your mind as you observe the children working and, in turn, can help to inform the 'Account' section. The comments you make in the 'Interpretation' section are based upon the observations in the 'Account' or, put another way, the 'Account' contains the evidence for your interpretation and assessment. Finally, the 'Action' suggestions rely on what has been said in both the 'Account' and 'Interpretation' sections. Let's consider some examples, keeping the importance of the relationship between the sections firmly in mind.

Lizzie was playing a base 10 version of the 'Fish Game' found in Nuffield Mathematics 2 (Figure 6.1).

The game is played by two children taking it in turn to spin (or to roll the die) and putting out the score obtained in fish. Whenever 3 fish are collected they are put into a net and the net is then placed in the correct column. Three full nets are loaded into a boat and the boat placed in the 'boats' column. The game need not be competitive, although children often point to a net and say, 'That one's mine.' The game ends when two full boats have been built up.

From time to time, the teacher may ask the children to put the appropriate numerals (0, 1 or 2) in the frames provided.

boats	nets	fish
1	1	2

'1 boat   1 net   2 fish'

From this, discussion can follow on the *position* of the numerals and *what they stand for*. 'The 1 on the left means 1 boat; the 1 in the middle means 1 net; the 2 on the right means 2 fish.'

The principle of exchange should also be discussed in simple terms. 'Three fish make a netful; three nets make a boatful.'

Figure 6.1 *The Fish Game (from Nuffield Mathematics 2 Teachers' Handbook)*

FORMATIVE TEACHER ASSESSMENT RECORD

Y1 ☐ Y2 ☐ Y3 ☐
Y4 ☐ Y5 ☐ Y6 ☐

Name: Lizzie T.   Date:
Activity: Place value exchange game - the fish game

Possible Outcomes

Knowledge of exchange of numbers, 10 units for one ten.
Language of exchange.
Counting in tens and units.
Understanding of place value.

Account	Interpretation	Action
Realised after adding on dice throws had 12 fishes - thought - "I'll change for a net as I've got two left over." Still adding all fish up every time. Not remembering how many had left & adding on dice roll. Lots of language of exchange - will swop for ten, change for a net. Has linked the nos. to tens and units because of base 10. When on 9 "I'll need one more to change for a ten." Got 2 on dice roll "I've got one fish left over". Said at end of game "three nets makes thirty and four in fishes column makes 34."	Lizzie has still got problems in the area of counting on - she still has to count on in ones from the start - has not yet become able to add on from the number last counted. Has a good grasp of exchange mechanism. Has got some idea of place value. Has some knowledge of number bonds to ten.	Needs practice in counting on from original number. Needs to work on number bonds to 10 and 20. Needs to have plenty of practice in above before moving to t.u. algorithms. Lots of practice in exchange games like this one - different bases also - move on to new game with tens and units as things to exchange.

Figure 6.2 *Completed Formative Teacher Assessment Record for Lizzie*

The 'Account' (Figure 6.2) gives a clear picture of what the teacher was able to perceive and to hear. Using direct quotes of things individual children have said is an excellent strategy and provides highly specific data for analysis. In Lizzie's case, the interpretations 'Has a good grasp of exchange mechanism' and 'Has got some idea of place value' can be seen to emerge from specific statements in the account (Figure 6.3).

Account	Interpretation	Action
Realised after adding on dice throws had 12 fishes - thought - "I'll change for a net as I've got two left over." Still adding all fish up every time. Not remembering how many had left & adding on dice roll. **Lots of language of exchange - will swop for ten, change for a net.** Has linked the nos. to tens and units because of base 10. **When on 9 "I'll need one more to change for a ten." Got 2 on dice roll "I've got one fish left over". Said at end of game "three nets makes thirty and four in fishes column makes 34."**	Lizzie has still got problems in the area of counting on - she still has to count on in ones from the start - has not yet become able to add on from the number last counted. **Has a good grasp of exchange mechanism.** **Has got some idea of place value.** Has some knowledge of number bonds to ten.	Needs practice in counting on from original number. Needs to work on number bonds to 10 and 20. Needs to have plenty of practice in above before moving to t.u. algorithms. Lots of practice in exchange games like this one - different bases also - move on to new game with tens and units as things to exchange.

Figure 6.3 *Interpretations emerge from the Account for Lizzie*

Danny was playing a base 6 version of the 'Fish Game'.

The bold sections in Figure 6.4 show how statements in the interpretation column emerge from statements in the account. In other words, the account provides the assessment evidence, as in the following example from Conor's record.

Conor has been playing a different place-value dice game with three other children. Each player has a score sheet with a number of boxes drawn on it (Figure 6.5). A caller throws the 0–9 die and the number called has to be entered in one of the four boxes. After four calls each player examines their score sheet. If the statement is true the player scores 2 points. The process continues until the score sheet is complete. Each player finds the total number of points scored.

64　EFFECTIVE TEACHER ASSESSMENT

FORMATIVE TEACHER ASSESSMENT RECORD　　Y1 ☑　Y2 ☐　Y3 ☐

　　　　　　　　　　　　　　　　　　　　　　　　Y4 ☐　Y5 ☐　Y6 ☐

Name : Danny　　　　　　　　　　　　　　　　　　　Date :
Activity : play the fish game in base 6

Possible Outcomes

Practise number bonds to 6
Experience of exchanging 6 fish for a net, etc.
Development of language of exchange
Understanding of place value
Counting on mentally

Account	Interpretation	Action
Danny played the game confidently from the start, swapping fish for nets and keeping a tally of his score. He chatted constantly throughout the game, pointing out who was winning, helping others. When he threw a 6 he picked up a net straight away "Oh yeah I can just pick up a net". "We've all got the same number of nets but she's got 3 fish". He counted on in his head except when he had 5 fish and threw a 5 - "That's 10" and took one fish away and took a net. "It's more important how many nets you've got."	Danny is confident and able to exchange, keeping a record of the numbers involved. He fully understands the concept of exchange. He realises that the first digit is the most important for the size of the number. He uses his number bonds to ten rather than counting on and shows he can handle subtracting and adding in his head. He used lots of language of exchange, showing a good grasp of the exchange system.	He is ready to move onto similar activities using base ten such as Unifix exchange h.t.u. game using h.t.u. mat. Danny could then move on to more formal tens and units activities and apparatus.

Comments :

Figure 6.4 *Completed Record for Danny*

---

1 | 6 | 4 |　<　| 7 | 3 |　　3 | ☐ | ☐ |　<　| ☐ | ☐ |

2 | ☐ | ☐ |　<　| ☐ | ☐ |　　4 | ☐ | ☐ |　<　| ☐ | ☐ |

Score 2 points for each true statement.

Figure 6.5 *Place-value score sheet*

Keeping an eye on what you say where!

Sometimes the boundaries between the 'Account', 'Interpretation' and 'Action' sections become somewhat blurred. Comments that are really meant to be actions end up as interpretations; or part of the account finds its way into the interpretation, or occasionally interpretations appear that do not seem to have any obvious relationship with the account at all! The distinctions between the sections will become more

---

FORMATIVE TEACHER ASSESSMENT RECORD   Y1 ☐ Y2 ☐ Y3 ☐
                                         Y4 ☐ Y5 ☐ Y6 ☐

Name : Conor   Date :
Activity : A group of 4 children play the Place Value game

Possible Outcomes

Assess the degree of place value concept. See how quickly he could make a decision. Is he prepared to take a chance?
To know value of a number in either tens or units place.
Fair play, keep pace, not to disturb others during play.

Account	Interpretation	Action
Played this game confidently. He made one mistake 94<75. Knew it was an incorrect statement. The 9 was thrown on the 3rd throw of the die and his two 'less than' boxes were empty. When challenged he answered straight away that he should have put it into the units to make 49. Says confidently in round 4 (33<55) after 3rd throw that he's going to win. In round 5 says "I won by 10 no, more than that."	He has a good idea of place value. He seems able to predict the likelihood of numbers coming up, e.g. most likely to win with a 33. Knows quickly 'greater' and 'less than' and in some instances by approximately how many.	Play game again and use 'less than' digits (if statement is correct) as score to introduce t.u. addition. Play 'Nasty Game' version of this game to test strategies and knowledge of place value to make others lose. Use expanded notation.

Comments :

This activity gave me a good indication of Conor's ability. He was well able to play fair and keep pace, but his enthusiasm led him to call out a little and may have worried the less confident members of the group.

Figure 6.6 *Interpretations emerge from the Account for Conor*

Account	Interpretation	Action
Realised after adding on dice throws had 12 fishes - thought - "I'll change for a net as I've got two left over." Still adding all fish up every time. Not remembering how many had left & adding on dice roll. Lots of language of exchange - will swop for ten, change for a net. Has linked the nos. to tens and units because of base 10. When on 9 "I'll need one more to change for a ten." Got 2 on dice roll "I've got one fish left over". Said at end of game "three nets makes thirty and four in fishes column makes 34."	Lizzie has still got problems in the area of counting on - she still has to count on in ones from the start - has not yet become able to add on from the number last counted. **Has a good grasp of exchange mechanism.** **Has got some idea of place value.** **Has some knowledge of number bonds to ten.**	Needs practice in counting on from original number. Needs to work on number bonds to 10 and 20. Needs to have plenty of practice in above before moving to t.u. algorithms. Lots of practice in exchange games like this one - different bases also - move on to new game with tens and units as things to exchange.

Figure 6.7 *Three positive achievements*

clearly defined as you develop your own skills of observation and analysis. It's important to remind yourself every now and then that the interpretations constitute your assessment and as such you are trying to identify positive attainment: what the learner knows, understands and is able to do. Reviewing the 'Interpretation' section of Lizzie's record reveals three positive aspects, although the opening comments in this section focus upon what Lizzie is *unable* to do (Figure 6.7). And with Dawn playing alongside Conor, the only mention of what she *is able to do* is found in the 'Account' section of her record (Figure 6.8).

The opening 'interpretation' on both Lizzie's and Dawn's record would be better reformulated under the 'Action' section. In fact, Lizzie's teacher picks up the area of 'counting on' in her first 'Action' recommendation: *'Needs practice in counting on from original number'*. Does it matter then, you might well ask, if the same thing appears twice on the record or if, as in the case of Dawn, the 'Interpretation' section slides into possible justifications as to why Dawn did not demonstrate many positive attributes on this occasion? One of the reasons why it

FORMATIVE TEACHER ASSESSMENT RECORD	Y1 ☐ Y2 ☐ Y3 ☐
	Y4 ☐ Y5 ☐ Y6 ☐

Name : Dawn   Date :
Activity : Place Value Game

Possible Outcomes

Assess the degree of place value concept. See how quickly a decision can be made. Is she prepared to take a chance?
To know value of number in either tens or units place.
Social demands: fair play, keep pace.

Account	Interpretation	Action
Dawn did not play this game confidently. **However she always read the actual number correctly.** There was quite a lot of hesitation and looking to see what others had written. In her 2nd go 79<54 the die scores were 7,9,5,4, she made poor decisions. She read statement as 79>54 even when challenged. In 54<47 having put 54 in < box she could have placed 7 in tens box as it was thrown third.	Dawn needs further practice in order to develop her concept of place value. She is not an unintelligent child but likes to be 'right' in what she does, therefore her hesitation could have stemmed from that. It was unfortunate (for her confidence) that all the others scored much better than she did. As the < was new to her she might have been confused by it.	1. Play this game again to see if further practice yields a better result. 2. Using cards and dice (0-9), draw out or throw 4 numbers, write them down as t.u. and add the < or > sign to make them correct. 3. Play 'Find the Pairs' game and t.u. Snap. 4. Games using different bases.

Comments :

This activity confirmed the feeling I had that Dawn was uncertain of place value. She needs to be given practice where she has to make a quick decision otherwise she will spend ages not wishing to make a mistake.

Figure 6.8 *Keeping an eye on what you say where – Dawn's achievement in the Account is not picked up in the Interpretation*

is important to clarify what to write where, and to stay with the principles behind the format, is the need to make the best possible use of time and energy. You need to be economical in the words that you use, but at the same time record enough to serve your purpose of being able to:

✦ identify what children are able to do, know and understand;
✦ make recommendations for future action;
✦ use the whole procedure to inform your classroom practice in the widest sense.

Account	Interpretation	Interpretation
Danny played the game confidently from the start, swapping fish for nets and keeping a tally of his score. He chatted constantly throughout the game, pointing out who was winning, helping others. When he threw a 6 he picked up a net straight away "Oh yeah I can just pick up a net". "We've all got the same number of nets but she's got 3 fish". He counted on in his head except when he had 5 fish and threw a 5 - "That's 10" and took one fish away and took a net. "It's more important how many nets you've got."	Danny is confident and able to exchange, keeping a record of the numbers involved. He fully understands the concept of exchange. He realises that the first digit is the most important for the size of the number. He uses his number bonds to ten rather than counting on and shows he can handle subtracting and adding in his head. He used lots of language of exchange, showing a good grasp of the exchange system.	Is confident Understands and is able to exchange Understands...' Knows... Can... Knows...

Figure 6.9 *Practising punchy Interpretation*

And all this in as concise a form as possible!

One strategy to help you on your way is to view the 'Possible Outcomes', 'Interpretation' and 'Action' sections as lists. This should help you to be direct and punchy. Reserve any continuous prose for the 'Account', and even there be as sparing as possible. A second strategy to support you in developing an apposite vocabulary is to make use of the National Curriculum documents and other sources of checklists, where some succinct phrases for describing children's learning can be found.

Spend a few minutes editing the extract from Danny's record (Figure 6.9).

A glance at Danny's 'Account' reveals that as he played the game he was helping others who were unsure of what to do. This aspect of his 'performance' was not recorded by his teacher in the 'Interpretation' section and there were probably very good reasons for her not doing so at the time.

Nevertheless, this example raises the issue of whether it is appropriate to comment on *how* children worked in the 'Interpretation' section of the record. If teacher assessment is to do with

+ providing information to help with planning learning experiences, and
+ providing information for parents and other interested bodies,

then including statements as to how children respond to particular activities, in terms of attitude and approach, seems eminently sensible. The only note of caution here is to look back to the 'first thoughts' exercise in Chapter 3, where it became clear that aspects of personality or social behaviours are often more easily and immediately identifiable, hence they can sometimes dominate assessment thinking. Effective teacher assessment does not ignore these domains but ensures that intellectual or academic attainment receives apposite attention. In other words, if when you glance at your list of interpretations you can't find references of the 'knows, understands or is able to do' kind, (and this would include statements such as 'is beginning to . . .' or 'has some idea of . . .'), then you need to do a quick rethink and check out your approach, preferably using a colleague as a sounding board.

Specifying action

❻ *The assessment that I did was of great help as it enabled me to pinpoint the exact level at which the children's knowledge of place value stood and therefore enabled me to move them on at a rate which was personally adjusted for them.* ❾

(Ruth)

Completing the 'Action' section of the Teacher Assessment Record seems to provide many teachers with that satisfying 'aha!' experience, as it becomes crystal clear that there really is something tangible in all this assessment work for both children and teachers. It's helpful to be as specific as possible in your recommendations for action, avoiding rather vague statements such as 'more practice with similar activities' or 'more experience of fair testing'. The resources available in your classroom can help to define the actions more closely. Notice how specific the Actions are on Dawn's Record. Working through possible action in this way can help you to identify gaps in your resources, both personal and material.

There will be occasions when you are not sure of the best possible course of action for an individual child or group of children, and discussion with subject coordinators or specialists will be your best bet. Of course, there's no guarantee that coordinators will always know which experiences to plan for next, but sharing a number of Formative Teacher Assessment Records with colleagues can help to sharpen the focus of professional development, promote some lively debate and bring some of those entrenched beliefs out of the cupboard for a dusting!

What story does Danny's teacher have about learning new ideas in mathematics (Figure 6.10)? There seems to be a strong

Possible Outcomes
Practise number bonds to 6 Experience of exchanging 6 fish for a net, etc. Development of language of exchange Understanding of place value Counting on mentally

Account	Interpretation	Action
Danny played the game confidently from the start, swapping fish for nets and keeping a tally of his score. He chatted constantly throughout the game, pointing out who was winning, helping others. When he threw a 6 he picked up a net straight away "Oh yeah I can just pick up a net". "We've all got the same number of nets but she's got 3 fish". He counted on in his head except when he had 5 fish and threw a 5 - "That's 10" and took one fish away and took a net. "It's more important how many nets you've got."	Danny is confident and able to exchange, keeping a record of the numbers involved. He fully understands the concept of exchange. He realises that the first digit is the most important for the size of the number. He uses his number bonds to ten rather than counting on and shows he can handle subtracting and adding in his head. He used lots of language of exchange, showing a good grasp of the exchange system.	He is ready to move onto similar activities using base ten such as Unifix exchange h.t.u. game using h.t.u. mat. Danny could then move on to more formal tens and units activities and apparatus.

Figure 6.10 *Using assessment to continue professional debate*

sense of commitment to working through practical activities in some kind of sequence. One of the exciting aspects of undertaking a close analysis of what you say about individual children is that it can help you review your own beliefs about teaching and learning and subsequently develop your own practice. In this particular example, this would involve checking out your beliefs concerning the place of practical activity, how and when it is appropriate and what alternatives there might be.

One of Danny's strengths is his facility to add and subtract in his head. What if his next learning experiences capitalised on this and moved him straight into adding larger numbers in his head, perhaps using the calculator as a starting point? How does this option compare to the one suggested above? (For the purposes of this exercise it's not possible to say you'd do both!)

Possible outcomes

As we saw in Chapter 5, the 'Possible Outcomes' section of the Formative Teacher Assessment Record considers the potential for learning inherent in particular activities or experiences. 'Possible Outcomes' reflect your planning aims. The richness of the learning activity in turn determines the possibilities for assessment. Much of the concern surrounding the early National Curriculum assessment requirements centred on the vast quantity of material to be assessed. Certainly the sheer volume caused considerable problems for the developers of standard assessment tasks at Key Stage 1, and contributed to a restricted range of material being asssessed by SATs. But any standardised assessment procedure is governed by all kinds of constraints, not least of which is the need for the assessment to take place within a specified period of time. Teacher Assessment is ongoing and has the advantage of being able to address the level descriptions across Key Stages. *'But, there's still a lot to cover!'*, you mutter through clenched teeth. Absolutely, but rich learning experiences are rarely confined to one aspect of learning or isolated aspects of attainment at any one time, as Ruth highlights:

❢ *The completion of the Possible Outcomes section was a catalyst to clearly define the aims of the activity and therefore the assessment. In doing so, it became clear that the aims of the activity were much wider than I had anticipated. I had seen this activity purely in terms of an assessment of their ability to exchange ten 'unit' items for one 'ten' item. When I examined my aims more closely, I found that the game also clearly exhibited their grasp of number bonds to ten and their understanding of the conservation of number. It also showed a vast amount of information about their personal and social relationships. . . .* **9**

Planning for learning–assessing

Taking planning for learning as your prime focus and allowing the assessment to 'fall out' of the learning experiences is one of the key principles for effective teacher assessment.

Ruth experienced how one activity can touch upon a number of aspects of attainment within one subject area. Other activities will range both across different level descriptions *and* across subject boundaries. In this way, over a period of time, you can ensure both coverage of the National Curriculum for learning as well as coverage for assessment requirements.

The exception to the rule!

Having spent some time emphasising that *learning* needs to be uppermost in your mind as the starting point for teacher assessment, it has to be said that there might be occasions where you start from the *assessment* perspective! The Formative Teacher Assessment Record in Figure 6.11 provides an example of an activity that was designed primarily as an assessment task, from which the teacher has been able to assess a number of attainments.

Adapting the Record format

The central purpose of the Formative Teacher Assessment Record is to provide a framework for looking at children's learning with the planning–learning–assessing dynamic in mind. Once you feel confident with the principles and structure that this particular format offers, you may wish to embellish the record to support your own style of working. The design used in the examples in this chapter evolved over a period of time, and along the way many teachers adapted the basic format to suit their own needs.

FORMATIVE TEACHER ASSESSMENT RECORD

Y1 ☐ Y2 ☐ Y3 ✔

Y4 ☐ Y5 ☐ Y6 ☐

Name : Marie   Date :

Activity : To find the weight of an unknown object

Possible Outcomes
The use of balancing scales Estimation 1 Kg = 1000g + and - as inverse operations Find the missing value

Account	Interpretation	Action
Used hands to compare the two tins. Thought the baked beans were heavier. Used balance to compare unknown tin with 1Kg. Suggested it was quite a lot less than 1Kg. Put both tins on together to balance 1Kg. Knew 1000g = 1Kg. Estimated answer.	Could use balancing scales to compare weights. Understands and estimates numbers up to 1000. Knows 1000g = 1Kg. Practically interpreted the task.	Provide further activities to ensure fuller understanding of inverse operations.

Figure 6.11 *An activity designed for particular assessment purposes only*

In the final example (Figure 6.12), Barbara chose to return to the 'Action' section periodically to *date* when particular recommendations had been followed through. At the same time, she attaches some of Ian's written recording as a representative sample of work. In this way Barbara begins to build up a portfolio of children's work which forms part of an overall Record of Achievement. The advantages of Records of Achievement for recording and reporting purposes are outlined in Chapter 8.

As long as the central purpose of looking at children's learning and the planning–learning–assessing cycle is retained, then almost anything goes in terms of making additions to the Formative Teacher Assessment Record format. At the same time, we would caution against making the Record unnecessarily complicated. At present the basic framework is designed to keep the focus very firmly on the task of assessing children's learning and using the assessment to plan future learning experiences. It's worth keeping a check on any changes you and your colleagues are considering by asking *'How is the change helping me in the task of assessing children's learning?'* and *'How is the change supporting me in the analysis of my own classroom practice?'*

USING THE FORMATIVE TEACHER ASSESSMENT RECORD 75

ODD and EVEN NUMBER PATTERNS

Draw a 4x4 grid and write in the numbers 1 to 16, in order. You may start wherever you like but the next number must be put in an adjacent square in any direction, but not diagonally.

Here are 2 ways of doing it but there are many others.

7	8	9	10		12	11	10	9
6	1→2	11			13	2→3	8	
5←4←3	12				14	1	4	7

Colour in
What do yo
Try it wit
Does the s
Try with o
What about
diamonds?
triangles?
hexagons?

FORMATIVE TEACHER ASSESSMENT RECORD   Y1 ☐   Y2 ☐   Y3 ☐
                                          Y4 ☐   Y5 ☐   Y6 ☐

Name: Ian B.   Date:
Activity: Odd and even number patterns

Possible Outcomes

Identify odd / even numbers
Understands odd / even numbers
Recognise patterns
Predict patterns
Hypothesise

Account	Interpretation	Action
"You say 1, 2, then every time you say 2, it's an even number... it's the second number each time that's even... For big numbers you look at the units. If they're even the big number is even."	Can identify and explain odd / even numbers. Can recognise and explain similarities between diamond / square grid and effects on results.	Provide opportunities to explore patterns that emerge in e.g. 100 squares compared with 100 triangles. 3/96 Provide opportunity for work to be extended in order to encourage further hypothesising and testing (e.g. triangle grids) 4/96
Explained pattern for diamond grid - 4 sides as in square. Understood that wider range of options on hexagon grid presented irregular / unpredictable patterns.	Worked systematically. Recognised when to abandon one aspect of task because outcome could not be predicted. Able to recognise factors which may affect likely results when predicting. Able to explain results.	Spiral patterns using 100 squares - including squares blocked off in centre. 5/96

Comments: Has worked for extended periods of time in 3/96 and 4/96 exploring other number patterns.

Figure 6.12 *Recording ongoing developments and attaching samples of work to the Assessment Record*

7 Organising for Effective Teacher Assessment

The approach to teacher assessment outlined so far involves systematic close observation and analysis of children's learning based on sampling throughout the Key Stage. On some occasions the assessments will stem from observing the children actually in action during an activity, but an equally valid approach is to 'closely observe' and analyse a piece of written recording or something the children have made. Using the Formative Teacher Assessment Record format enables you to have some idea, prior to observing, as to what you might see or hear (possible outcomes), and the observations you make form the basis of a written account of the children's actual responses. The assessment emerges as you interpret the account you have written, and the final stage in the planning–learning–assessing cycle is to consider the next step in the children's learning programme.

Ensuring time and space for close observation within the confines of a working day involves giving some consideration to organisational frameworks that support the observational process. In other words, if you need ten minutes of uninterrupted time in order to observe a group of children working, then it makes sense to establish uninterrupted time as an integral feature of daily routines and the general classroom ethos. But don't put off beginning to observe until you've created the 'right' ethos (you'll never get started!): both can develop alongside one another – the important thing is to make a start.

This chapter highlights two areas of classroom management that can be usefully revisited and fairly immediate action taken in order to enhance the potential for daily teacher assessment. On another level, we then go on to consider two more fundamental aspects of classroom life that can be reviewed *at some point* during the learning–assessing cycle as part of the ongoing development and refinement of 'good enough' assessment practice – that is, classroom practice that supports children's learning.

Establishing a supportive classroom ethos: sharing responsibility with children

If commitment and energy are to be given to reviewing classroom practice in order to ensure a working environment that enhances learning–assessing and, in particular, close observation, then it's as well to keep some of the advantages of taking time to observe children in mind. Fiona comments:

❢ *By closely observing children I get to know the children so much better. Recording my observations in my markbook at random moments wasn't nearly as effective. I also kept a ticklist which had to be filled in periodically. Sometimes, by the time I got to filling them in, I had forgotten what I had seen the children do.* ❥

And Y5 teacher, Wendy:

❢ *Before using this system [Formative Teacher Assessment Record format] I found myself being obsessed with assessment, wanting to give them a test on this and that. I got so anxious about assessing children that I started collecting tests and ideas to assess them. Now that I have had time to reflect on what I was doing, I am sure I was over-assessing them, if that is possible! Instead of helping the children to learn better, my assessment panic must have interfered with their learning.* ❥

Keeping a sense of perspective about assessment is one of our recurring themes, and Wynne Harlen (1983) offers a comforting image in this context:

❢ *Assessment in education has been criticised for interfering with learning, the analogy being that of a gardener constantly pulling up his plants to see if the roots are growing. There is some truth in this, particularly if there is too much assessment of the wrong kind, but it also distorts reality to make a point. Gardeners do have to find out if their plants are growing and they do this, not by uprooting them, but by careful observation with a knowledgable eye, so that they give water and food at the right time and avoid either undernourishment or overwatering.* 9

Nevertheless, it has to be said that the thought of beginning 'careful observation with a knowledgeable eye' can be somewhat daunting and raises some immediate concerns:

- My children are too young to be left to themselves.
- My class is too noisy.
- There are too many interruptions to the day.
- I'd rather be teaching.
- My children don't work in groups.
- I have no time to observe children.
- Where do I find good activities?
- My room is too small and cluttered.

At this point it's probably a good idea to write down your own immediate response to the thought of observing a small number of children during the day and then play devil's advocate with yourself, or ask a friend to play the role, something along the following lines:

I'M TOO BUSY TEACHING TO OBSERVE.   Isn't observing part of teaching?

OKAY, BUT THE CHILDREN NEED ME.   What exactly do they need you for?

WELL, I HAVE TO ORGANISE THINGS.   What 'things' in particular? Can the children do some of this?

Looking 'underneath' the original statement helps to unearth and review some of the underlying principles as well as assumptions that influence what you do in the classroom.

Revisiting classroom practice in this way provides the starting point for developing a classroom ethos that supports close observation and, in turn, the close observations help to inform and influence future practice. In many ways there's something of the chicken and egg situation here, but there is one key aspect of classroom management to consider in the context of making close observation and assessment possible in the classroom: sharing responsibility with children.

Fiona, the class teacher of twenty-eight ten-year-olds, states that since she started discussing the Formative Teacher Assessment Records with the children they have behaved more responsibly. For example, Fiona believes that they don't interrupt her if she is with a group of children:

> *I don't think it is pure coincidence that the children have become more responsible at the same time as I started my close observation sessions. Either it was because I myself got better organised and that had a knock-on effect on the children's attitudes or they felt they had to take learning more seriously because they were being assessed.*

Tina, a class teacher of eight-year-olds, had a similar experience. She told her class that she was going to spend some time working with one group of children to make some notes about how they were doing. She promised that she would tell them what she had found out about their work. Tina explained:

> *I didn't expect them to be so cooperative. I told them if I had my notebook with me that meant I was writing things down about them and if it wasn't terribly urgent they were not to interrupt me. Initially they did interrupt after five minutes. It meant constant reminders, but then I could observe for longer and longer periods of time. This is very good training for them, because even at other times of the day they are becoming more and more independent.*

Angela offers the following advice to her colleagues:

> *I grouped the rest of the class into mixed ability tables so that the more able could help those who were less able. I told the children that they could ask each other for help before they came to me. I explained to them that I was working with a small group today, and that their turn would be on another day. I was pleasantly surprised at how well the class got on with their activity and how helpful they were to each other. I have been encouraging this kind of collaboration more since*

then and I find that life is easier for us all. And, above all, there is much more of a positive atmosphere of learning in the classroom.

The extent to which you share responsibility with the children for both learning–assessing and the smooth running of the classroom is inextricably linked with your personal vision (theory) of the role of the teacher which, in turn, can help or hinder observation and the learning–assessing cycle. Considering the following aspects of classroom management can get you started on a review of classroom practice with 'sharing responsibility with children' as the connecting thread:

- structuring the day/week, and
- organising resources.

Structuring the day/week

Although it is not possible (nor desirable) to make the working day longer, it *is* possible to consider ways of making more efficient use of the time that is available in the classroom. In Chapter 4 we suggested you look at your daily timetable to identify sessions throughout the week where it would be possible to observe and make some notes. At the same time, you might like to take a fresh look at how each day or week is structured. It's easy to fall into following a pattern of doing things in a particular way and for certain organisational traditions to be followed because they have always happened that way. 'Story' at the end of the day for younger children would be an example of one such 'tradition'. Other examples would be playtimes, assembly times, PE slots and access to computer facilities. The advent of the National Curriculum has given birth to some new conventions, yet it's worth juggling daily/weekly timetables in a variety of ways to see which structures create productive slots of time that both enhance children's learning and enable you to undertake some close observation. Find a colleague and share routines together. Keep asking *'Why do we structure this part of the day in this way?'*, *'What if we tried it this way, what would the knock-on effect be?'* At the same time, reflect upon the way that additional adult support – for example, classroom assistants or parents – can be best utilised. Inevitably there will be certain constraints which help to define the range of possibilities, but looking at alternative approaches to organising periods of time and sharing resources helps to ensure that basic organisational structures provide optimum support.

Organising resources

Attending to the arrangement of material resources in the classroom helps to reduce the amount of time spent responding to the following kinds of interruptions from children:

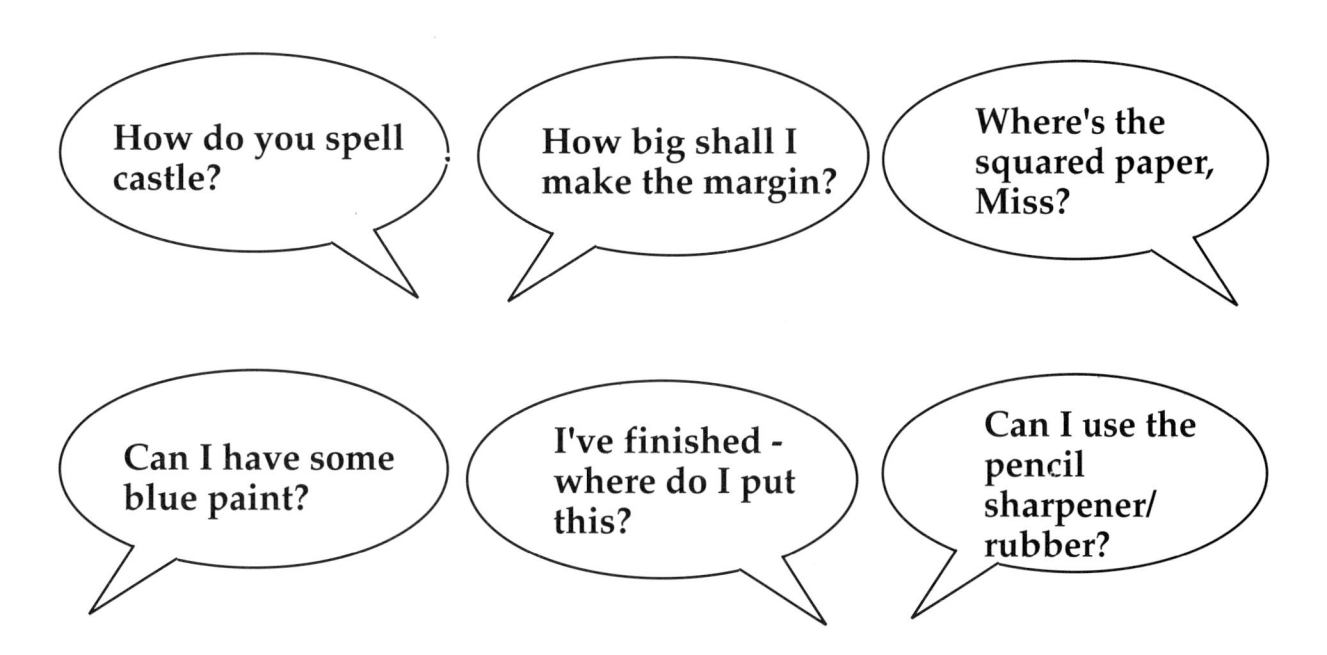

How do you spell castle?

How big shall I make the margin?

Where's the squared paper, Miss?

Can I have some blue paint?

I've finished – where do I put this?

Can I use the pencil sharpener/rubber?

Looking at the classroom from a child's point of view can be very revealing. Are cupboards and shelves easily accessible? Are shelves, trays and cupboards labelled?; materials and books coded in a way that minimises the need for children to come to you for basic materials? Is there an overabundance of tables, chairs or cupboards which hampers movement and restricts your own access to observing particular groups of children? Involving the children in some of the decisions as to what goes where in the classroom pays dividends in the long term! The fifth in-service session outlined in Chapter 9 is designed to help focus attention on alternative classroom layouts. Meanwhile, training children to use dictionaries, word banks and reference materials, or leaving the editing of doubtful spellings till later, stressing the importance of uninterrupted working time, valuing draft work and encouraging children to view mistakes and imperfections as an important part of learning, can all contribute towards children taking more responsibility for their learning. At the same time, personal projects and investigations provide a rich source of activity for children to return to throughout the week, and encourage children to take some initiative in planning, deciding and organising what to do next.

Discussing the entries on a Formative Teacher Assessment Record with children can let them in on the secret that 'what do I do next?' is informed by 'what I know, understand and can do *now*'. Involving children in the planning–learning–assessing cycle in this way enhances self-assessment skills and encourages children to make decisions and choices for themselves as to what to do when they 'finish'. This in turn releases you from certain kinds of interruptions for short periods of observation time.

Taking assessment on to a broader view of teaching

In primary classrooms a whole range of different kinds of activity will be on offer to the children at different times throughout the day and week. Part of classroom life involves fairly routine work as well as high-powered new learning activities. As you discuss your observations on the Formative Teacher Assessment Record with children, you can help them to recognise the purpose and function of particular activities. You can also share the fact that your own role and participation changes and differs according to the nature of the activity being worked through at any particular moment in time.

Helping children to construct their individual list or programme of ongoing practice work, as well as areas for further development, helps them towards recognising when it's appropriate to have some expert input (from yourself) and when it's a case of thinking things through for themselves. Sometimes it is the teacher and not the learner who ends up doing most of the 'work' for a particular activity, hence the feeling that there's 'no time' for observing and assessing. Encouraging children to view their learning as problem-solving changes the teacher–learner dynamic somewhat and releases you to make contributions that are highly focussed on learning needs, as opposed to dealing with more mundane queries concerning pencils and rubbers (although there will always be some of the latter!). Establishing a working pattern whereby children are clear that it is their job to do the thinking and learning involves checking out both what's on offer and how you make your expectations explicit to the children. It is possible that you intend one thing to be happening but the intention gets lost somewhere in the translation into classroom activity. In this context it's worth reflecting upon: the nature of the starting point for learning, and your personal style of intervention and interaction.

The nature of the starting point for learning

In the planning–learning–assessing model (day-to-day learning activities) the focus for assessment and the need to design special assessment tasks is the exception rather than the rule. The assumption is that an activity with rich learning potential will inevitably create an assessment opportunity. In this way, teacher assessment takes place at different points *throughout* the learning cycle and not just at end-points. Deciding which activities are 'rich in learning potential' can be helped by checking out whether the activity exemplifies at least some of the following qualities. The activity:

+ provides children with a challenge;
+ has potential for developing in a number of different directions (open-ended);
+ has potential for crossing subject boundaries;
+ leaves room for children's contributions;
+ can offer different things at different levels;
+ promotes discussion;
+ has potential for children to work in a variety of groupings: individually, pairs, small groups, large group;
+ has clearly identifiable content and process (purpose and function).

You might want to add more points to the list by looking at some of the activities you use with children and considering which features contribute towards making the activity a worthwhile learning experience.

Styles of intervention and interaction

Monitoring the kinds of intervention you make is part of reviewing everyday practice. Research has demonstrated that teachers do much of the talking in classrooms. Redressing the balance by providing children with more opportunities for talking together is one strategy and involves looking at the starting point on offer in the first instance. Another strategy involves exploring your personal intervention style in terms of listening and responding to children. Use inset session two in Chapter 9 to help you focus in on your personal style. Try out different kinds of interventions and make a note of the range of effects upon learning: assessing can be a salutary but worthwhile experience. Reflecting upon the kinds of interventions you make helps to uncover how you view the teaching–learning process and your image of yourself as a teacher; both influence how you organise and manage your classroom as a learning environment.

For teacher assessment purposes it is not essential to maintain the invigilator's impassive omnipresence: silent and devoid of body language. Asking open questions, responding to children's statements with *'tell me more . . .'* and posing additional problems for the children during an activity not only enhances the learning but also the assessment potential of the activity. Any interventions you make do not immediately invalidate the assessment, but become a natural part of the whole procedure: part of the context. Things you say and do can be noted in the 'Account' which informs the 'Interpretation' and recommendations for 'Action'. The legacy from past assessment practices, whereby assessment was seen as a special kind of activity usually at the end of a learning sequence and requiring distinctive behaviours on the part of learner and teacher (the former usually being required to work in silence on a special task and the latter relegated to policing and marking duties), is hard to shake, as illustrated by Barbara:

❛ *Because of serious confines of space within my working environment, it is impossible to assess how much a child may have 'borrowed' from the words/ideas of others when responding to direct questions.* ❜

And Ruth:

❛ *I obviously was not able to give them help in playing the game (although I was itching to do so!) but I also wanted to help them assert themselves, as Jagruti was totally dominating the group and was not letting Poonam, a quiet child by nature, participate in the game to any great extent.* ❜

The underlying concern for both Barbara and Ruth is that the assessment will not be 'accurate' or 'fair' in one way or another. Barbara is concerned that children will use ideas from each other and not their own (is this cheating or learning?!), and Ruth indicates that some children will dominate a group activity and prevent others from showing what they can do.

In Chapter 4 we suggested that instead of searching for the perfect assessment scenario (could there ever be one?), a more productive approach for all concerned, and one which allows for the conflicting demands of learning and teaching, is to focus on fair and accurate *enough* assessments in which the *context* of the assessment defines both the extent and limitations of each assessment. This is not to suggest that teacher assessment will not be rigorous or valid. Rather, it is an approach that enables you to recognise any assessment for what it is and to get started on assessment with some reasonable expectations of both yourself and the whole procedure in mind.

Reflecting upon her own initial approach to assessment, Barbara commented:

> *I had feared that the less confident of the children would seek help from or copy others in the group, and that my assessment would not, therefore, be 'fair' or 'accurate'. I had made a mistake which I imagine will be common to many teachers involved in similar forms of assessment, in that I had changed my normal practice of working. In general terms, I am not over-concerned about children copying during the initial stages of commencing a task. I believe that children learn much from watching and emulating, and can gain the confidence to tackle an activity which they might otherwise – for a variety of reasons – find difficult.*

> *Equally, the children in my class know that I value individuality very highly, and will not accommodate situations where one child produces work for others to reproduce. Once I have established my own framework of values with a class, I find that children rarely abuse the facility to gain ideas or help from others.*

Ruth's description of her non-intervention in the game involving Poonam and Jagruti provides another example of how the thought of assessing children causes quite a significant change in teacher behaviour. The influence that assessment has on daily practice needs to be far more subtle, and to originate from the central theme of enhancing learning opportunities by sharing the responsibility for learning–assessing with children.

In summary:
At one level it is important to make management and organisational choices that support formative teacher assessment as an integral feature of teaching and learning. Viewing learning and assessing as a shared responsibility with children is a useful guiding principle in this context.

On another level, making teacher assessment effective in terms of enhancing children's learning requires a commitment to an ongoing review of personal practice in at least two key areas: the choice and nature of activities on offer to children throughout the curriculum; and the range and quality of teacher intervention and interaction.

8 Sharing Assessment with Parents: recording and reporting

Chapter 1 outlined the statutory requirements governing the kinds of information schools need to make available to parents on an annual basis. This chapter explores the use of the Formative Teacher Assessment Record for reporting achievement to parents within the context of individual Records of Achievement throughout the primary school.

The Regulations stipulate the *minimum* written information that parents are entitled to receive. The form and the style of the report remain open to interpretation, although the development of Records of Achievement has always had the support of official agencies such as the DFE and SCAA:

A Record of Achievement is a cumulative record of an individual child's all-round achievement. It records positive achievements and ideally involves children, teachers and parents in the process of its production.

(DES Circular 8/90)

Deciding how to present written reports which are accessible and meaningful to parents and remain manageable within the context of all the other demands on teacher time is no easy task.

In order to gain some insight into the task of providing information to parents in written form, we take a look at how three parents reacted to the reports they received at the end of a school year. The parents were interviewed within three weeks of receiving the reports. Extracts from the interviews and reports are presented and used as a focus.

Interview 1

Sally has two children in the same school. She received reports for both of them from their respective classteachers. Her son John is nine years old and her daughter Emma is six. When asked how useful she found the reports, Sally replied that they were quite different:

Emma's report:

> English
> Emma has a good understanding of spoken English. She enjoys listening to adults reading to her, especially adventure stories. She answers questions and participates actively in discussions. She has good pencil control. Spellings seem to be more phonetic, but I only correct the mistakes one or two at a time so that her imaginative writing is not discouraged.

John's report:

> English
> John has produced some good work this year. He tries very hard but his handwriting lets him down. His presentation needs improving. Writing does not come naturally to John, though he tries hard to produce some stories. His reading is average for his age.

Sally: As you can see, Emma's report is very useful, not because it says good things about her, but because it gives me a very clear picture of how she is doing. It tries to pinpoint her strong points and what needs more attention. It tells me more about her. For example, I can get her adventure books, help with her spelling. But John's report does not tell me much except that his handwriting is appalling, though the teacher puts it much more kindly and mildly. What about his spelling? His imaginative writing?

Interviewer: Did you meet the teacher before you received the report?

Sally: Yes, very briefly at the parents' evening at the beginning of the year. With so many parents waiting, we did not have much chance to talk.

Interview 2

The second interview was with Glenys, mother of eight-year-old Michael.

Michael's report:

> Science
> Michael has contributed well to some science experiments this year. He has worked reasonably well but could do much better and achieve a higher level than he has at present.

Interviewer: Have you had school reports for Michael before?

Glenys: Yes. We have always had a school report. They were no use in the past.

Interviewer: Why is that?

Glenys: I never found them useful. When they used to send reports home saying 'Michael could do better' I wanted to scream and ask, better than who, what and so on. This year in the report 'could do better' has a whole load more meaning.

Interviewer: Tell me more. In what way is it more meaningful?

Glenys: You see, I see Michael's teacher a lot more this year. Once a term I have a conference with the teacher. She discusses Michael's work with me and shows me some of his work. I tell her what I think is important about Michael and . . .

Interviewer: And what?

Glenys: She discusses the National Curriculum syllabus with me. I see what his age group could be doing. First I couldn't take it all in. Now I am beginning to have a good idea. When I see 'could do better' I know exactly what she means.

Interview 3

The third interview presented here is with David, father of nine-year-old Thomas.

Thomas's report:

> Mathematics
> Thomas enjoys Mathematics. He has a good understanding of mathematical concepts. His problem-solving and investigational skills are improving. His process skills are also developing well. He shows leadership qualities.

Interviewer: Have you always had school reports?

David: No.

Interviewer: Are you pleased that you have them now?

David: No.

Interviewer: Explain why you said no. It was a quick no.

David: It's because it's no use to me. What does it say? I don't understand what she is saying for a start. Is he learning his tables? Is he doing his mental arithmetic? How fast does he work? Is he accurate? Instead of these, here is a load of words. Only God knows what they mean. I feel completely shut out by the school.

Each interview highlights the desire of the parents to receive more detailed information concerning their child's progress and achievement. The interviews point toward a need to provide information that goes beyond generalisations, uses an accessible vocabulary and makes links with the National Curriculum.

Beyond generalisations

Reports need to pinpoint both achievements and areas for future development. The contrast between John's and Emma's reports illustrates this aspect. Emma's report provides the parent with some points for action, whereas she feels that John's is too vague and leaves her lost and helpless. If you look at the report again, 'John has produced some good work this year' does not tell the parent very much about John's writing. The fact that the parent has not *seen* any of John's work makes it even less informative.

Accessible information

If we look at the third transcript, Thomas's father, David, is clearly frustrated with the amount of technical vocabulary in his son's report, not really understanding the terms 'process', 'investigations', 'concepts' and so on.

Not only the terms but also the significance of the words in an educational context are unfamiliar to him. Based on his own school experience, David expects a report covering his son's knowledge of multiplication tables and his ability in mental arithmetic tests. In order to share current practice and enable parents to engage fully in home–school partnerships, it is essential to communicate to parents changes in the curriculum, different approaches to teaching and other developments in school practice.

Making links with the National Curriculum

Michael's report, although on the face of it somewhat vague, is still helpful to his mother, Glenys. It becomes accessible to her because of the termly meetings she has with the teacher. During these meetings – 'conferences', as the school refers to them – the teacher explains the National Curriculum targets and other technicalities in the context of Michael's learning. This makes the whole process of Michael's education more accessible to her. She does not feel that school is a place where mysterious things happen, in which she has no part to play. Offering more than generalisations, developing a shared vocabulary and making links with the National Curriculum emerged earlier in Chapter 3 in the context of developing some working principles for assessment. If assessment, recording and providing information to parents are seen as a cycle (Figure 8.1), then it follows that some of the principles that inform practice in one element of the cycle will inform practice in either or both of the remaining elements.

Records of Achievement (see page 97) are a means to bring together schools' policies and practices on assessment, recording and reporting into a coherent whole. The Formative Teacher Assessment Record mirrors this same process and provides a structure for observing, assessing, recording and reporting achievement. As part of the overall Record of Achievement, the Formative Teacher Assessment Record can

assessing achievement → recording achievement → reporting achievement → (cycle)

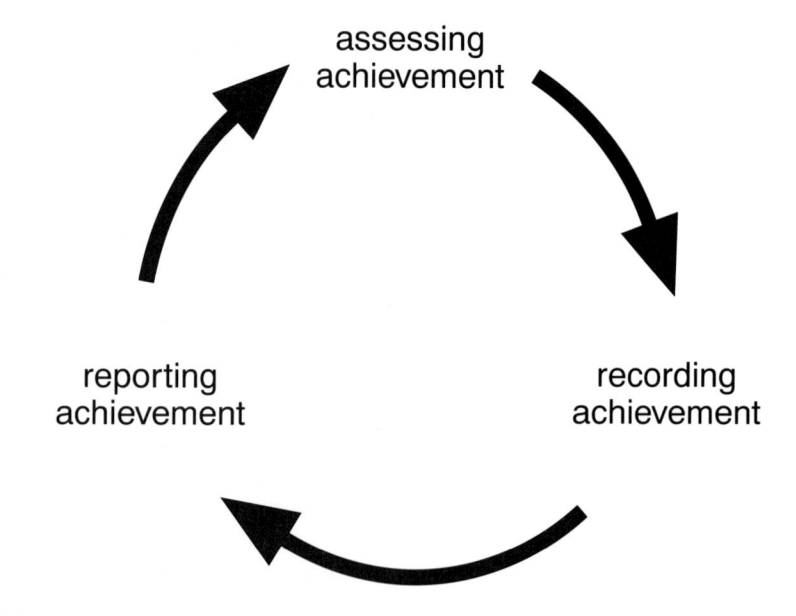

Figure 8.1

provide an accessible and manageable focus for meaningful dialogue between parents, children and teachers.

Using the Formative Teacher Assessment Record as part of a record-keeping package

As well as providing a structure for assessing children's learning, the Formative Teacher Assessment Record – as its title suggests – serves as a record of your assessment of children's learning. One overriding concern expressed by teachers in relation to record-keeping is the time needed to complete records and the number of National Curriculum subjects to cope with.

In Chapter 4 we established that record-keeping needs to follow on from teacher assessment. With this in mind, the Formative Teacher Assessment Record was designed primarily to provide a structure for making sense of observations and completing teacher assessments, but the need to record and report assessments influenced the final design choice. The format serves the dual purpose of enabling teachers to communicate readily different aspects of children's achievement, to parents and children, as well as supporting teachers in their analysis and assessment of children's learning. The Record establishes what children know or understand within a particular context, and the 'Account' section provides the evidence for the assessment.

Looking at children's learning in this systematic way needs to be balanced against the other demands of classroom life. Hence this approach to teacher assessment is firmly based upon *sampling* children's learning. A careful analysis of one observation can provide a wealth of assessment information, as the examples in earlier chapters and the Appendix illustrate. Sampling in this way will not necessarily cover the complete content of the programmes of study, but neither is it expected to do so! So, where is all this leading and how does it help to meet the National Curriculum assessment requirements? Let's revisit the requirements, taking the current procedures for Key Stage 1 as a model.

A *summary* of each child's attainment in the National Curriculum subjects is required at the end of the Key Stage. The Formative Teacher Assessment Records will include some interpretations that relate directly to the National Curriculum level descriptions. As you identify the particular elements of the programmes of study by means of the sampling process, you can record them on to a separate record that can act as a transition point to the final summary at the end of each Key Stage. This should help in the process of finding the 'best fit' level descriptions required by the National Curriculum, for each child.

The format for what can be viewed as a *Summative* Teacher Assessment Record would consist of an 'expanded' listing of the programme of study (PoS) content statements. When preparing such a list, you will find it helpful to relate the PoS statements to the statements included in the level descriptions, as a guide to continuity and progression. When you feel confident that the Formative Teacher Assessment Record has identified a particular element of the programmes of study, you can highlight the relevant part on the summary chart.

The summary chart, listing the separate elements of the programmes of study and with highlighted areas showing where a child has displayed 'understanding', moves with the child from class to class and could be used from the Reception year onwards. In this way, a summary of attainment is built up throughout the Key Stage and a number of teachers contribute to the developing profile. Y2 and Y6 teachers will have the extra task of translating appropriate information from the school summary chart to the formal end-of-Key-Stage Teacher Assessment record, although if the class records are up to date, there is no reason why this task could not be completed by administrative staff.

The Formative Teacher Assessment Record will not provide

evidence of *all* the children's attainments throughout the Key Stage, but it will provide a goodly number and at the same time enhance your skills of observation and interpretation – which in turn will make any 'on the hoof' assessments you make during daily classroom interactions effective and incisive. Assessments made other than using the Formative Teacher Assessment Record procedure, can of course be recorded *directly* onto the summary chart. Sometimes you will have tangible evidence to accompany the assessment (products and artefacts) and sometimes not – it's the quality of the assessment that counts, and not the volume of materials available to support each assessment. Establishing how much evidence it is reasonable to have at your fingertips is part of developing a whole-school policy. It might be useful to keep the following in mind as you discuss the possibilities:

✦ evidence *enough* (as opposed to enough evidence!);
✦ pupil portfolios as part of a Record of Achievement.

It is neither essential nor sensible for every entry in a record-keeping system to be supported by tangible evidence that is filed away for future reference – classrooms across the land would be bulging at the seams! In the course of using the Formative Teacher Assessment Record to structure her observations and assessments, primary teacher Rachel began to reconsider her own approach to evidence collection:

❢ *I have always felt that evidence collection to support assessment is one of the more positive aspects thrown up by the ERA. We have certainly welcomed it warmly at school. We have spent a lot of time reducing evidence collection to reasonable and storable levels. Thinking through 'positive assessment' has however caused me to rethink my evidence collection. It does have a role to play, but one that is far removed from my initial judgement. Evidence collection provides a chart of past progress. This is of use to identify the child's varied and unique progress through their schooling. It can provide a history of, for example, areas in which confidence has always been lacking, and be used therefore as a diagnostic tool in investigating why a child finds subsequent learning in an area to be problematic. It is however limited, as is all history, by its context. It is a reflection, however carefully selected, only of that child's working at a specific time, in a specific area of work, with a specific teacher, within, in fact, a great number of constraints. It provides welcome evidence for us as teachers to confirm that our children have progressed. This does however call into play a certain amount of generalisation.*

❛ *I still feel that evidence collection has a degree of validity, but I am beginning to recognise its limitations in a more dynamic and positive approach to assessment. For assessment that is ongoing and developmental, as I believe all assessment should be, the implication is that evidence collection has limited application.* ❜

You might like to use Rachel's statement to focus discussion with colleagues about evidence collection to support assessment.

From recording to reporting

Providing a written report of individual achievement across a range of National Curriculum areas and other activities for 30+ children is a lengthy and time-consuming activity. The style and format of the written report becomes fairly crucial, given that on the one hand parents would like to know more about their children's progress, and on the other hand there are limits to the amount of time it is sensible for you to give to this kind of activity. Using the Formative Teacher Assessment Record as a focus for reporting is offered here as a starting point for your own school-based discussions. Involving parents in the development of reporting procedures adds a vital ingredient to the whole process; as the audience for written reports, parents can offer particular insights and perspectives. At the same time, parents can be given a sense of some of the dilemmas facing schools within the context of assessing, recording and reporting individual achievement.

One school presented the Formative Teacher Assessment Record to parents during an assessment workshop and asked them to assess four children and fill in the record. Amongst other things, this served to familiarise parents with the requirements of the National Curriculum programmes of study; but perhaps more importantly, it gave some insight into the complexity of assessing children's learning.

Using the Formative Teacher Assessment Record for reporting to parents

A collection of Formative Teacher Assessment Records and accompanying summary charts could constitute the major part of a written report for parents of Y1, Y3, Y4 and Y5 children, presented as an integral part of a Record of Achievement that details children's achievement in activities outside the National Curriculum. In this way, the 'report' is written and collected together over a period of time as an integral part of the assessment procedure, and not compiled as a précis of achievement at the end of the school year. This approach uses the Formative Teacher Assessment Record as a central feature of each element of the assessment, recording and reporting cycle. Time saved in not writing additional material to summarise achievement (it's already available in the Formative Teacher Assessment Record and summary charts) can be given to parent–teacher conferences or parent–teacher–child conferences, where the discussion is highly focussed on specific aspects of children's learning identified through and recorded on the Formative Teacher Assessment Record. An overview of progress to date is provided by the highlighted summary charts. These charts have the advantage that the programmes of study for each subject are actually visible for parents and teachers to share and discuss together.

In order to report the results of statutory standard assessments (Y2 and Y6) and in order to share the remaining information required by the assessment regulations for all year-groups, it will be necessary to have one additional sheet which can be completed at the time of issuing the report. Many local education authorities have a standard format for this purpose, detailing the individual's attendance record for the year and giving levels of attainment for the individual with comparative information about the average levels of other children in the school at the end of the same Key Stage. In addition, for those children who have undertaken standard assessment tasks, information needs to be given as to the results of the arithmetic, reading and spelling assessments.

The combined elements of the Formative Teacher Assessment Record and summary charts do not have the shape and form of traditional written reports, but when time is at a premium, thinking creatively about forms of reporting is essential. This approach to reporting satisfies a number of important criteria:

- it is accessible to parents;
- it goes beyond generalisations;
- it provides a focus for home–school partnerships (the 'Action' section on the Formative Teacher Assessment Rec
- explicit and meaningful links are made with the National Curriculum;
- effective use is made of teacher assessment, and time is use efficiently.

The Regulations governing reporting stipulate that parents are entitled to receive a written report by 31 July of each year.

This does not necessarily imply that reports must always issue at the end of the summer term. Whilst reports on end of key stage assessments will necessarily have to issue late in the term, schools may wish to adopt different schedules for reports in intervening years. This is a matter for schools' discretion within the terms of their overall assessment, recording and reporting policies.

(DES Circular 8/90)

Using the Record as part of a Record of Achievement approach to reporting means that reporting for R, Y1, Y3, Y4 and Y5 *can* readily take place at times other than the end of the school year. This is an option worth some consideration, as the summer term can become rather full with other aspects of school life and colleagues will then be more able to support Y2 and Y6 teachers during the national assessment period.

Records of Achievement

Since the introduction of the National Curriculum and Statutory Orders for reporting children's progress, many primary schools have been developing Records of Achievement for their children – an initiative which has been successful in many secondary schools in recent years. A Record of Achievement is described as:

A file or a folder including various assessments of the child's work, skills, abilities, personal qualities. Within the school curriculum as a whole, it gives details of achievements both inside and outside the classroom. It can also include a portfolio of samples of the child's work. A Record of Achievement, which is sometimes called a profile, forms the basis for the summary report which is needed each year.

(DES Circular 8/90)

Within a Record of Achievement it is possible to recognise that:

- ✦ Children learn at different speeds; their abilities, achievements and development are not fixed.
- ✦ Learning is not confined to the cognitive dimension: social interactions, personal interests and motivation all play their part.

- Children learn more effectively if they know what is expected of them.
- Self-assessment compels children to reflect on their achievement and review progress.
- Children, teachers and parents can all contribute to the Records of Achievement. This partnership is a very powerful one, which enhances effective schooling.
- Concentrating on positive achievements enhances the child's self-esteem and gives greater incentive to succeed.

One approach to the Record of Achievement

Right from the start, we decided that if we were going to have Records of Achievement, it will be devised by us for our school. The support documents from the central agencies helped to provide a general framework, but we produced a system which was workable for us. And, of course, one which would not add to the workload. We discussed details such as storing and presentation for consistency of approach.

(Primary school assessment coordinator)

In this particular school each child's Record of Achievement is divided into three parts. Part One contains admission records, medical records, notes about family background and any other confidential records. This is stored in a secure place in the school office, and only teachers have access to this part of the record. The other two parts are ongoing, continuous records. Part Two mainly consists of assessment records: Formative and Summative Teacher Assessment Records with National Curriculum statements highlighted or pencilled in, and children's work relating to it attached, together with any checklists, SATs assessments, LEA tests and transcripts of any recorded conversations. These records are discussed with the children and are also referred to at meetings with parents. This part of the Record of Achievement is filed away by the teacher in a cupboard.

Part Three, called the 'portfolio', is an A4 ringbind folder and looked after by the children. They have complete responsibility for keeping it in order and sorting work out periodically. When the folder gets too bulky, some pieces of work are sent home. Pat, a Y5 class teacher, explained:

This process was initially time-consuming and chaotic, but children soon got used to it. They used to drive me up the wall wanting every piece of work in the folder. It took a while. Now I think introducing this was one of the most exciting parts of the Records of Achievement policy. The difference in children's attitude to their work is incredible and you have to be here for a few days to appreciate the real power of it. **9**

We looked at several children's portfolios. The contents varied a great deal between different children. We asked children how they selected pieces of work for their portfolios and were given the following responses:

> **'I choose anything I am pleased with'**
> *Sasha, 8 years*
>
> **'I put in things which please my mum and dad.'**
> *Sarah, 8 years*
>
> **'I choose work which my teacher likes; when she puts "well done" or something like that. Sometimes if she says "that is good work" I put that work in as well.'**
> *Emma, 10 years*
>
> **'I choose everything which makes me clever.'**
> *George, 8 years*

We saw several pieces of work in the portfolios. The older children had dated the work and some had written comments on their work. The younger ones had smiley faces and short comments describing what they thought of their work.

Misa, in the Y5 Junior class, showed us her portfolio with great pride. The contents included: written work, problem-solving activities, home-made maths games, photographs of a bird table she had constructed with a group of children in her class, a photocopy of her swimming certificates, a press cutting of her involvement in fund-raising activities for a local charity, and her end-of-term science assessment (Figures 8.2 and 8.4).

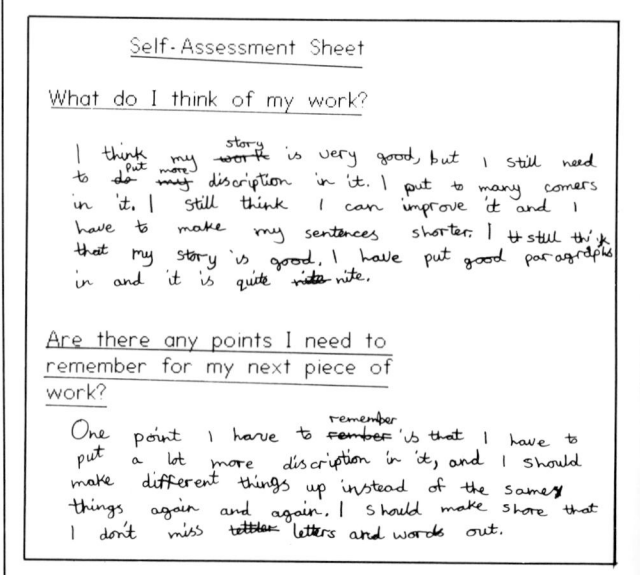

Figure 8.2 *Misa's story and her assessment of it*

Seven-year-old Rowena showed us her 'best story', which was going to an exhibition, and her assessment of it (Figure 8.3).

Other portfolios contained self-assessment and assignment sheets such as Diane's computing sheet (Figure 8.5).

Practical organisation of portfolios

Most classes stored the portfolio in large tidy-boxes or trays which were placed in an easily accessible place. Children were responsible for handling their own portfolios. We specifically asked the teachers if they had any problems with the organisation. For example, we asked about additional workload and were told:

SHARING ASSESSMENT WITH PARENTS: RECORDING AND REPORTING 101

> The girl who ran away
>
> One day there was a girl called Lucy. She lived with her mum and dad and brother. One morning Lucy woke up and went to school. But when she got there evry body was being horrible to her even her best friend Emma. That night when evry body was asleep she creped out of the house and she ran away to her faviret ant's house when she got to ant's house on the door step she found a key she went in side and foud a box she put the inside the key hole and opened it in it there was a newspaper on the first page there was a thing about this ant wick had been kild in a car crash. A cople of days later she found it was her ant that had been kild in the crash and went back home. When she went back to school all her friends had missed her and her family and her best friend emma said she wouden't be horrible to her agin.
>
> THE END

> Self Assessment Sheet
>
> What do I think of my work?
>
> I am plesed with and it is one of the best pices of I have done and riten in my file and I think it is very good.
>
> Are there any points I need to remember for my next piece of work?
>
> Well I think I have to remeber some more spellings and rememeber to put comers and follstops.

Figure 8.3 *Rowena's story and her assessment of it*

No more than before. Part One of the Record of Achievement was always there. We always kept private records. Part Two, the observation sheets and other teacher assessment evidence, helps us to get to know the children so much more, it is continuous assessment and ... the Portfolios – after the novelty and excitement at the initial stages, now children look after it anyway.

Initially, teachers had to spend a considerable amount of time discussing with the children how to select pieces of work for their folder; that the individual folders were confidential and should only be looked at by the teacher and child concerned; and that the children themselves were responsible

102 EFFECTIVE TEACHER ASSESSMENT

> My Science work.
> Name. Misa Patel Class..5K Date………
> 1. How do you think you have done in science this year so far?
>
> I think I have done very well ~~during~~ this past year. Sometimes not knowing what I am doing but that is soon delt with. All in all I think I have done very well.
>
> 2. Which activities have you enjoyed the most?
>
> The best activities I have enjoyed ~~un-enjoy~~ most is when we had to taste food and gess what it is and gess what drink we're ~~your~~ drinking.
>
> 3. What have you not enjoyed?
>
> I have not enjoyed the bit when we had to write about what we did.
>
> 4. Write comments about your general progress, as you see it.
>
> I think I have made alot of progress in my work. I have made progress in writing more and ingessing things and when I have to work with a partener. When I go to see things about sience I take more notice.

Figure 8.4 Misa's assessment of her science work

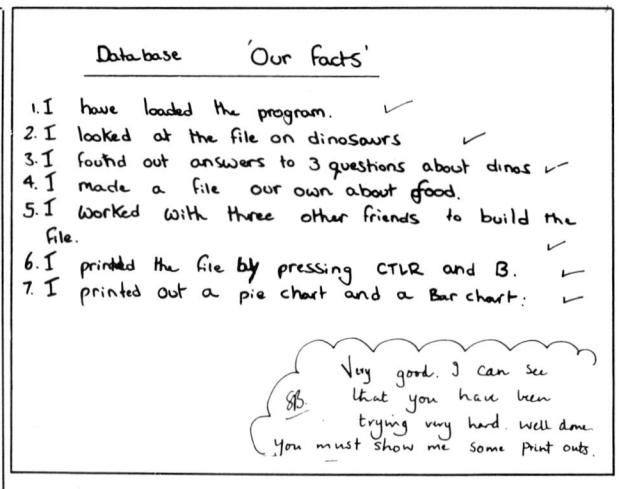

> Database 'Our facts'
>
> 1. I have loaded the program. ✓
> 2. I looked at the file on dinosaurs ✓
> 3. I found out answers to 3 questions about dinos ✓
> 4. I made a file our own about food.
> 5. I worked with three other friends to build the file. ✓
> 6. I printed the file by pressing CTLR and B. ✓
> 7. I printed out a pie chart and a Bar chart. ✓
>
> SB. Very good. I can see that you have been trying very hard. Well done. You must show me some print outs.

Figure 8.5 Diane's assessment of her computer competence

for keeping the folder tidy. As the system became a natural part of classroom life, children were observed behaving more responsibly and a calmer ethos permeated the classroom.

The headteacher commented that teachers were involved in careful monitoring of the range of work undertaken by the children, as some children were reluctant to produce work in areas in which they were either not very interested or not very competent.

What are the benefits of children having their own portfolios?

We asked the teachers what they thought the benefits were in children having their own special portfolios. The list is compiled from different teachers' comments:

+ It is very motivating for the children.
+ The portfolio celebrates a child's achievement.
+ There is a strong element of self-assessment in the selection of work.
+ This helps children to be self-critical; it also helps to set targets to be achieved.
+ It gives the teacher a framework of reference for discussion with parents – helps them to use a language they understand, because it is 'real' work.
+ Children quite often do work or finish pieces of work at home. Sharing this with the parent, and discussing it, makes the parents more aware of the school's ethos and philosophy.
+ It encourages children to strive for high quality and have higher expectations of themselves.

All three parts of the Record of Achievement (with the second and third part carefully selected) go with the child to the new class teacher and eventually the new school at school transfer stage.

9 Developing a Whole-School Approach to Assessment

❛ *Whole-school policies on assessment, recording and reporting are one of the keys to good and consistent practice. They offer individual teachers a sound framework for development at classroom level.* ❜

(*ERA*: DES Bulletin, Issue 4)

A school policy on assessment should explain the philosophy, aims, objectives and procedures agreed by staff regarding the assessment of children. Some teachers ask:

❛ *With all the literature sent to schools, why do we need to reinvent the wheel, talking about assessment and spending our valuable time on it . . . can't we just read all the bits and someone else puts a statement together?* ❜

In this book we have emphasised the need to work through and move towards a *shared* approach and understanding of the assessment process.

Successful implementation of effective teacher assessment lies in a shared ownership of process and procedures. As one teacher explained:

❛ *I was totally miserable about the whole business of assessment. I felt I didn't have the training at college or anywhere to have the expertise to make judgements about children's learning. During the compilation of a school policy on assessment, the staff talked and talked; when the policy was finally put together, I felt I didn't even need it, I felt so much more confident. The whole assessment procedure made sense and I wondered why nobody ever insisted on all this before. I am even being very creative about assessment and recording now.* ❜

Devising a school policy: What needs to be done?

A school policy does not have to be a very lengthy document, but it needs to take into account the needs of the children in your particular school. The contents of the policy should underpin all the assessment procedures in the school and any observations related to assessment should be fed into curriculum planning and organisation. This then provides a sound basis for teaching and learning within the school.

Although it should not be the responsibility of the assessment coordinator (if you have one) to write a policy on assessment, she has an important role to play in planning for it to happen. She is the person who can organise meetings, liaise with LEA advisers and take the responsibility for drafting documentation.

The whole process of planning and devising the policy should take place over a period of time. Principles of assessment should be tried, discussed and reflected upon. Rushing the initial process may result in the document being inaccessible and ending up discarded in the teacher's drawer.

A plan of action

1 Reviewing the requirements.
2 Where are we now?
3 Establishing principles.
4 Drafting the policy.
5 Evaluating and reviewing.

1 Reviewing the requirements

Gather all the SCAA, DFE and LEA documents and books on assessment together and display them in an easily accessible place. Give yourself a deadline for reading them! Alternatively, work in pairs: each person reads a piece of documentation and reports the essence of the materials to the other partner.

2 Discussion: Where are we now?

The data we presented in Chapter 2 demonstrated that teachers are at different stages in their thinking about assessment. Some consider record-keeping to be assessment. Some don't consider that formal assessment is necessary at all. Some teachers consider administering the LEA end-of-year test paper is the only assessment required. Some have always observed continuously and recorded findings regularly. Individual teachers also have their own private ways of recording children's progress in markbooks.

Discussing the question *'Where are we now?'*, can lead you to reflect on the prior question of *'What do we understand by teacher assessment anyway?'* Providing prompt cards with questions as starting points for the discussion of 'where we are now' is a useful strategy:

✦ How do you assess children now?
✦ How do you record children's progress?
✦ Do you discuss your assessment with the children?
✦ Are children involved in their own assessment?

3 Establishing principles

This stage may take several sessions but is often considered by many teachers to be the most useful for their own professional development.

Sharing the exercises in the earlier chapters of this book (especially Chapter 3), would provide one way in for this session.

Alternatively, focusing on these questions can get you started:

✦ **Why** do we assess children?
✦ **When** do we assess them?
✦ How do we gather **evidence** about children's learning?
✦ **How often** do we assess children?
✦ How do we **record** what we find out?
✦ How are **children** involved in their own assessment?
✦ What kind of **classroom organisation** would support effective teacher assessment?
✦ What provisions are there for ensuring **equal opportunities** in assessment for all children?
✦ Who will have **access** to the records?
✦ How will **parents** be involved?
✦ How will the assessment be **reported**?
✦ How will the policy on assessment be **evaluated and reviewed**?

4 Drafting the policy

After all the discussions, this stage should be simpler and should not take too long. It is helpful to present your draft policy to a probationer from another school or a final-year initial training student or a parent and ask them to comment on how useful and accessible they find the policy. After all, the policy must make sense to new members of staff, parents and governors. One school we visited during this stage had a role-play session. Teachers paired up, one in the role of the assessment coordinator and the other taking the role of a teacher who has just been recruited as a new member of staff to the school straight from initial training. This resulted in a whole range of issues being clarified and the final document providing a much more helpful framework.

Evaluating and reviewing

If a policy is to remain effective it needs to be regularly evaluated and reviewed. A useful strategy is to view any policy as a draft. Subsequent redrafting is based on putting each draft into practice and using the experience to inform the new draft. In this way principles and practice can be reformed and reshaped and respond to the needs of individual school contexts, as well as attend to any new legislation. Establishing an evaluation and review timeline and including minor and major review points would be essential. Minor review points can take place at any time in the year when practice indicates that there is a need for changes to the policy. An example of a major review point would be to identify one year-group and follow it through to the end of a Key Stage. The assessment experience of the cohort throughout the Key Stage can then be used for the major review.

As we have emphasised throughout the preceding chapters, assessment practices take time to develop and refine. A vital step in this whole process is to work with colleagues in a mutually supportive way, trying alternatives, and discussing the advantages and disadvantages for you in your particular school context. In this way you will give yourself the necessary background experience to enable you to make informed decisions and choices about effective teacher assessment for the children in your care. In the following section we offer some starting points for inservice sessions to help you begin.

Continuing Professional Development: Some suggestions for inservice sessions

These sessions might form the basis of the third stage of developing an assessment policy: establishing principles and practice by trying out and reviewing the experience. All these ideas have been tried throughout inservice sessions with groups of teachers and schools across the primary phase. Six sessions are provided, but it does not mean that you should be using all of them. However, session one sets the scene and a personal agenda for the participants, and as such provides a useful introductory session. For each activity, aims, procedures and some questions to guide the discussions are presented in that order.

Session One: Setting my personal agenda

Aims

To provide an opportunity for teachers individually to air their concerns about assessment. This session acts as a personal reflection time, and gives teachers an opportunity to discuss their anxieties and apprehensions with their colleagues. It is also the time for participants to take a personal responsibility to use future sessions to develop their knowledge, skills and confidence in undertaking effective teacher assessment.

Procedure

Each member is given an assessment notebook to be used for all the sessions. (A4 size, home-made, with fifteen sheets of plain paper.)

Stage 1

Divide the first page vertically into two parts. On the left-hand side write down all your *concerns* about assessment issues (privately, for five minutes) and leave the right-hand side blank, using more than one sheet if needed. It may look like this:

DEVELOPING A WHOLE-SCHOOL APPROACH TO ASSESSMENT

CONCERNS	
I am very unfamiliar with terms used, the jargon	
I am not an expert.	
Primary teachers don't have the expertise.	
What tasks do you use for assessing children?	
Are we going to get some records from the authorities to fill in?	
When do I get time to assess, with all the other things I have to do?	
Am I going to get the sack if my children don't pass?	
How do I assess the ESL children?	
Who will mind the rest of the children while I assess?	

Stage 2 (in pairs)

Talk to your partner about one or two of your concerns for three minutes. Why is it a concern? Have you thought what's behind the concern at all? Are there any solutions your partner has already thought of? Where and to whom might you go for help?
 (Now, reverse roles.)
 Take two minutes to jot down anything which helped you from the brief discussion. An example is:

| I am not an expert. | After the discussion I see that my partner is in the same boat. I don't feel so bad now . . . we've also discovered we do have the expertise to make a start, at least. |

Stage 3

Each pair then joins another pair and discusses their points of concern. Again, take a further two minutes at the end of this discussion to jot down any more ideas that occurred. Share your thoughts.

Filling in the right-hand side of this exercise is an ongoing procedure that can take place at any point during subsequent sessions. It can be used by participants to evaluate where they are in their understanding of teacher assessment, both during and at the end of a series of staff development sessions. The notebook provides a focus for personal action and reflections.

Session Two: Listening and talking to children

Aims

The aim of this session is to help the teacher to reflect on her style of verbal intervention with children and to consider listening and questioning skills in the context of learning–assessing.

In preparation for this session, each teacher should be asked to bring with her a tape recording of a three-minute unedited conversation between her and a child about an aspect of mathematics or science. The aim of the interview/conference with the child is to find out what the child knows and understands in relation to a particular aspect of science (e.g. electricity) or mathematics (e.g. addition/multiplication of numbers). Three copies of the transcript of the interview also need to be brought to the session to share with colleagues.

Procedure

In groups of three, listen to the tape with the transcript in front of you. Do not interrupt the tape; make notes while you listen. After listening to the whole tape, discuss in your group what you have written down. Back in the large group, discuss some of the other points which have arisen for you during the exercise:

Who was doing more of the talking? Child or teacher? What kind of listener are you?
What kind of feedback was given to the child?

DEVELOPING A WHOLE-SCHOOL APPROACH TO ASSESSMENT 111

1. B: What's 18+18?
2. F: (Long Pause, looking down)
3.   36.
4. B: Good. How did you do that?   open question
5. F: I add 15 and then I kept on   working from what he knows
6.   counting until 18.
7. B: Right, and so you ...
8. F: And then 15+15, 16+16.
9.   17+17, 18+18.
10.   Right, OK. What is 24+24?
11. F: 48.
12. B: You did that quickly. How   is speed essential?
13.   did you do that one?   open question
14. F: I added two twenty's and two using knowledge of tens & units
15.   fours.
16. B: Right. What is 10?
17. F: 204.
18. B: How did you do t
19. F: I added two hu
20.   two twos

33. B: Well done. What about 28-9?
34. F: 19.
35. B: How did you do that one?   Mis-heard answer, therefore probed
36. F: Mmmm..   open question
37. B: Can you think how you did
38.   it?
39. F: (Long Pause)
40.   Did you count back?
41. F: Yeah, I counted back.   closed question
42. B: what you counted back 28,   short uninformative answer
43.   27, 26 in your head?   closed question
44. F: Yeah.
45. B: Can you think of another   uninformative answer always seems
46.   way you could have done it?   to be the result of my closed
47.   Do you know an easier way?   questions
48.   you might have done it?   open question
49. F: 19+9 is 28 and 28-9 is 19.
                                     knowledge of commutative law

Figure 19.1 *Interview with Faisal (Y4)*

How probing were the questions you asked?
What did you find out about the child? What does the child know? Understand?
What about attitudes? thought processes . . . ?
What kind of questions did you ask? open/closed? What are the implications of asking the child 'what do you mean by that?', as opposed to 'very interesting, tell me a bit more'?
What are the implications of different interview styles?

Lastly, on your own and taking no more than six minutes, write down what you have found out about:

- Yourself as an interviewer.
- The child's understanding of concepts, attitudes, processes, etc.

This should form the basis of some very fruitful discussion about the role of listening and talking to children.

Session Three: Observing children

Aims

To practise assessing children by observing them. How observing children can inform the teacher of different facets of the child's learning. To raise issues about the need for a structure for observation, and to highlight issues of management and organisation in the classroom.

In preparation for this session, teachers need to be asked to observe four children on an everyday learning activity using the Formative Teacher Assessment Record. They should bring four Records to the session with the 'Possible Outcomes' and 'Account' sections only completed. This task should be done in the normal classroom setting.

Procedure

In groups of four, teachers share their observation sheets and their experiences in carrying out the observation. Again, as a group, discuss the possible content of the 'Interpretation' and 'Action' sections. (Use Chapters 5 and 6 to help with this.) Discussion might focus on:

Benefits and difficulties of close observation for teacher assessment.
Aspects of classroom organisation to support effective teacher assessment.
The range of resources or new resource implications to enable appropriate 'action' to be taken.

The kinds of learning activities on offer in classrooms.
When and how does the teacher intervene?
How easily can links be made with National Curriculum statements of attainment?

Session Four: Moderation

Aims

To discuss the role of moderating assessed pieces of work and looking for agreement in assessment criteria. To explore how a shared meaning can be found through the moderation process.

In preparation for this session, teachers are asked to bring to the meeting three samples of children's written work. No names or ages are to be revealed.

Procedure

During the session teachers are asked to sort the pieces of work into groups and explain the criteria used. Debates and discussions are likely to be very powerful before any agreement is reached. After sorting the work, teachers may be asked to discuss and come up with the 'best fit' level description for a child and to consider what future action would be appropriate for that particular child.

The final part of this session is to focus on the benefits and any possible problems of teachers moderating each other's assessment. The following list was compiled during one such inservice session.

Moderation with my colleagues:

- helps me to share with others what they are doing;
- helps me with planning future action;
- brought the staff together to evaluate children's work for the first time in my school;
- made us all supportive of each other;
- increased my confidence.

Some teachers admitted that initially it was a highly anxious time, not to mention time-consuming, but nevertheless very worth the effort.

Session Five: Organising the classroom environment for assessment

Aims

The aim of this session is to look at ways in which teachers might organise their timetables and the physical arrangement of their classroom in order to support the observation and assessment process.

Teachers are asked to bring to this session a copy of their timetable and a plan of their classroom.

Procedure

During the first part of the session, in groups of four each teacher presents her timetable and a basic plan of her classroom, with separate cut-out mock-ups or representations of cupboards, desks and large equipment.

In the second part of the session, attention is given to classroom layouts. Continuing in groups of four, each plan is considered and alternative layouts suggested, 'tried' and discussed. Ways of organising basic classroom resources in order to support learning–assessing provides the focus for comparing and evaluating the different options.

Things to consider when re-arranging the classrooms could include:

- ✦ If taping children working together is one possibility for assessment, is there a quiet area in the classroom for this?
- ✦ If I need to work fairly quietly with a group for short periods of time, is there a comfortable space to do so with the rest of the class still within vision at a glance?
- ✦ Do children have safe access to basic working tools? a paper store? scissors? equipment? the computer?

A reflection time follows for each teacher to determine their own personal plan of action by listing three changes they can implement tomorrow and three longer-term changes that they may like to work on over a period of time.

Session Six: Keeping records

Aims

To evaluate existing record-keeping systems and to develop a set of principles about record-keeping.

In preparation, teachers are asked to bring to this session the records they keep about their children, if any.

Procedure

During the session, in pairs, teacher A is asked to talk to her partner about a child chosen by teacher B. Teacher A needs to show evidence for the comments she makes from the record examples. A and B change roles. This could be a depressing beginning to the meeting, but very powerful principles about record-keeping emerge! Questions arise relating to the usefulness of keeping records alongside discussions of different formats, style, content issues and self-assessment.

At the end of the session, a list of criteria for record-keeping systems can be made and the role of Records of Achievement considered.

Appendix

The following four completed examples of Formative Teacher Assessment Records illustrate how the format can be used to structure observation and assessment across a range of curriculum areas. You may choose to discuss each example with colleagues after reading Chapter 6, *Using the Formative Teacher Assessment Record*. The following features of the particular examples might be useful starting points for discussion.

The science example makes explicit reference to the National Curriculum programmes of study. What are the advantages and disadvantages of cross-referencing in this way? The teacher not only records Eleanor's individual responses, but also includes comments on how the group worked together on the activity. To what extent is it possible to dip in and out of observing the group and individuals within the group working on an activity? How much does the nature of the activity itself affect your observations?

Some of the responses by Chris in the 'making bags' activity demonstrate his scientific knowledge of materials. This illustrates how observing one activity can provide assessment opportunities in several subject areas. In what ways could you capitalise upon this?

In the mathematics example, a difference in Johanna's method of working on this occasion is noted by the teacher in the 'Comments' section. The somewhat tentative conclusion (viz . . . ?) acts as a useful reminder to the teacher that he might need to confirm this on a future occasion. On what basis will you feel sure *enough* about your assessments? Is it possible to establish a shared approach with colleagues on what counts as enough evidence? If the 'Account' section of the drama activity contained more detail, such as examples of things Yasmin had said, then the evidence for the 'Interpretations' would already be recorded. What are the difficulties of writing down children's talk as it occurs in the classroom? To what extent have you noted differences in the way girls and boys approach particular activities?

FORMATIVE TEACHER ASSESSMENT RECORD

Y1 ☐ Y2 ☐ Y3 ☐

Y4 ☑ Y5 ☐ Y6 ☐

Name: Eleanor   Date:

Activity: Which concrete is the strongest? How will we find out?

Possible Outcomes

Linking use of concrete to its properties
Devising and carrying out a fair test for testing strength of concrete made previously
    PoS Experimental & Investigative Science 1a, b, c, d, e
    PoS Materials and their Properties 1 and 2

Account	Interpretation	Action
Discussed physical properties of concrete 'ingredients'. "You need to add water. If you used it for a house it's not suitable, it's too crumbly." Discussed a testable idea, "If you drop them, the lightest will break." Worked through the idea that weight wasn't relevant with the group. Tested strength by dropping masses. Varied height and assisted to see the need for a fair test. Later discussed needing to keep the height the same, "Because it's fair."	Understands use of concrete as building material. Prediction made while trying to isolate variables Attempts at isolating the variable. Series of related observations made while testing.	Uses of other building materials, e.g. water-proofing. Discuss and evaluate the need for a fair test. Further practice devising and carrying out a fair test.

Comments:

Contributed to many parts of the discussion and made many suggestions. Some testable ideas but not able to verbally follow these through. Evidence of understanding fair testing through practical demonstration needed.

FORMATIVE TEACHER ASSESSMENT RECORD

Y1 ☐ Y2 ☐ Y3 ☑
Y4 ☐ Y5 ☐ Y6 ☐

Name: Chris
Date:
Activity: Making Bags

Possible Outcomes

Pre-design discussion
Predicting which materials to use
Estimating the amount of material
Estimating shape and size
Post-design discussion
Testing, modifying.

Account	Interpretation	Action
Chris decided not to work with another child, he wanted to make his own bag. Chris and Martyn decided what they were going to draw on the bags. Chris then drew his plan- decided not to have handles Chris decided upon cloth as he felt it would be strong. Drew a basic rectangular shape, cut it out and used it as template. Used staples- didn't work, so he sewed it. Decided to use masking tape to make sure it would not tear. Eventually made handles from stronger material. Tested with potatoes.	Understood that cloth was stronger than newspaper, plastic etc. Seemed not to need discussion as he knew what to do. Was able to estimate, cut and sew two pieces together.	Discuss with Chris the advantages of planning with a partner and sketching several possible designs before beginning work. Ask Chris to review his original design and justify both his modifications and way of working. Explore his knowledge of different ways of joining.

Comments:

FORMATIVE TEACHER ASSESSMENT RECORD

Y1 ☐ Y2 ☐ Y3 ☐

Y4 ☐ Y5 ☐ Y6 ☑

Name : Johanna   Date : ....

Activity : To find the area of a pentagon

Possible Outcomes

Ability to draw a hexagon
Understanding that area = space shape covers
Sensible application of known facts and skills (previous knowledge was how to find the area of a square, rectangle and rt. angled triangle)
Measuring
Multiplication, addition and division

Account	Interpretation	Action
Johanna decided that she was confident enough to work directly on file paper. She drew the pentagon to the correct size. Measured 5 external lines and horizontal internal line. Added the six measurements together (the perimeter of the pentagon plus one internal dividing line between the quadrilateral and the triangle. Gave this total answer as cm² (area).	Johanna can identify and draw a pentagon (knows the number of sides). She can measure accurately. She can add accurately. She was aware that the shape was less familiar than squares or triangles, so she adapted it internally - split it into squares and triangles.	Differentiation between area and perimeter must be made. Discuss practical examples in classroom, playground. Encourage awareness of value and influence of lines enclosing shape and those helpful internal lines. Discuss next piece of work with her as her work proceeds.

Comments :

Johanna usually checks her methods of working with me before she commits herself to paper - this time she didn't ... ? She must have been sure she knew what to do.

EFFECTIVE TEACHER ASSESSMENT

FORMATIVE TEACHER ASSESSMENT RECORD

Y1 ☐   Y2 ☑   Y3 ☐

Y4 ☐   Y5 ☐   Y6 ☐

Name: Yasmin   Date:

Activity: Drama with R.E. element of farmyard rules.

Possible Outcomes

Listening and speaking
Putting over a point of view
Convincing, elaborating
Adapting and adjusting
Collaborating

Account	Interpretation	Action
Repeated story in her 'case against the rat". Listened to cat's case so she could defend her own. Defended her case in a logical manner. Imagined her 'baby' chickens were getting muddy and told this to the cat. She wrote a letter into the scene to try to make the farmer read it and believe her. In the trial, clearly expressed her point of view (in role), and was convincing and persuasive. As the trial proceeded she adjusted the story (although at first stuck to the original). She saw boys making the story up and then she made up her own.	Can listen in group activities including imaginative play. Listens attentively and responds to stories. Listens to instructions. Can talk about story. Can listen to other children and adults, responds to questions and comments on what has been said. Can participate as a speaker in group activity and imaginative play. Can describe an event to the teacher / group. Can answer questions in role (asking questions did not arise). Uses imagination in developing an idea.	Provide opportunities for Yasmin to ask questions both in and out of role. Discuss with the whole class the different approach to developing the story taken by girls and boys. Check out whether the children perceive certain 'rules' for participating in this kind of activity.

Comments:

Bibliography

Association for Science Education (1990) *Teacher Assessment: Making it work for the Primary School*, ASE.

Barrs, M. *et al* (1988) *The Primary Language Record Handbook for Teachers*, Centre for Language in Primary Education.

Barrs, M. (1990) *Words not Numbers: Assessment in English*, National Association of Advisers in English and National Association for the Teaching of English.

Clemson, D. and Clemson, W. (1991) *The Really Practical Guide to Primary Assessment*, Stanley Thornes.

DES (1988) *National Curriculum: Task Group on Assessment and Testing: A Report*, Department of Education and Science.

DES (1991) Circular 14/91 *The Education (National Curriculum) (Assessment Arrangements for English, Mathematics and Science) (Key Stage 1) Order 1991*.

Desforges, C. (1989) *Testing and Assessment*, Cassell.

DFE (1992) Circular 5/92 *Reporting Pupils' Achievements to Parents*, Department For Education.

DFE (1995) Circular 1/95.

GAIM (1988) *Graded Assessment in Mathematics*, Macmillan/NFER-Nelson.

Galton, M. and Harlen, W. (editors) (1990) *Assessing Science in the Primary Classroom*, Paul Chapman.

Harlen, W. (1983) *Guides to Assessment in Education: Science*, Macmillan/Nelson.

ILEA (1980) *Checkpoints*, Harcourt Brace Jovanovich.

ILEA (1985) *Everyone Counts*, Harcourt Brace Jovanovich.

Johnson, G. *et al* (1992) *Primary Records of Achievement*, Hodder and Stoughton.

Mitchell, C. (1991) 'Planning, Learning, Assessing', Document 12 in *Mathematics in the Primary Curriculum* (E627), Open University.

SCAA (1993) *The National Curriculum and its Assessment* (Final Dearing Report), December 1993.

SCAA (1995) *Planning the Curriculum at Key Stages 1 and 2*.

SEAC (1990) *A Guide to Teacher Assessment* Packs A, B and C.

SEAC (1992) *School Assessment Folder 1993*